TORU DUTT

THE PIONEER SPIRIT OF INDIAN ENGLISH POETRY

A CRITICAL STUDY

K.A. Agrawal

ATLANTIC
PUBLISHERS & DISTRIBUTORS (P) LTD

Published by

ATLANTIC

PUBLISHERS & DISTRIBUTORS (P) LTD

7/22, Ansari Road, Darya Ganj,
New Delhi-110002
Phones : +91-11-23273880, 23275880, 23280451
Fax : +91-11-23285873
Web : www.atlanticbooks.com
E-mail : info@atlanticbooks.com

Branch Office
5, Nallathambi Street, Wallajah Road,
Chennai-600002
Phones : +91-44-64611085, 32413319
E-mail : chennai@atlanticbooks.com

ISBN 978-81-269-1078-6

Printed in India at Nice Printing Press, A-33/3A, Site-IV, Industrial Area, Sahibabad, Ghaziabad, U.P.

Preface

The dawn of Indian Independence has ushered us in an altogether changed political and social atmosphere. We are now proud of our nation and have begun to free ourselves from the glamour of the West, and study our customs, traditions, literature and culture with a sense of awe and admiration. This revival of interest in Indo-Anglian literature is a direct offshoot of a changed atmosphere. Indo-Anglian authors are now studied with pleasure and profit both in India and abroad side by side with their English and American counterparts.

Of all the Indo-Anglian authors, Toru Dutt stands out as a poet. A Hindu by birth and a Christian by education, this illustrious daughter of Bengal, while waging a grim yet heroic battle against her delicate health and foul disease started a hectic literary activity by the sweep of her imagination. She wrote very fast, as may be gathered from the fact that within a space of three years she produced no fewer than four literary volumes, nothing to speak of her long illuminating essays, letters and translations of speeches in French. She perhaps heard (as Lowell surmises) what Keats did, a voice urging 'what thou doest, do quickly' and when her dear sister, Aru, died of consumption like her only brother, Abju, she became almost certain that she would also meet the same fate. Thereafter, she, like Keats again, began working with all the restless energy of a haunted creative writer.

But it is strange that such a dedicated soul should long be remembered only for her *Savitri* and shorter poems. And it is quite surprising that she is regarded today, by a certain coterie of critics, as 'a dead horse', not worthy enough to be 'flogged' by a serious student of Indo-Anglian literature. The present study attempts to point out that Toru's other poems, too, have much merit in them and that she is still very much alive through her inspiring work. Her total poetic output has been fully analysed here in order to ascertain her position in Indo-Anglian poetry.

Toru's contribution to Indo-Anglian literature as a whole is noteworthy. In fact, entire structure of this brand of poetry is based on her solid achievement. She was the first Indian writer to handle English verse with ease and command. Her poetry may be meagre in bulk, but it is of permanent worth and this makes her at once the 'first major poet' in Indo-Anglian literature.

This study lays emphasis on the poetic aspects of Toru's writings. The events having a direct bearing on her poetic prowess and psyche have also been taken into account. Consisting of eight chapters, the book makes a detailed investigation into the nature and scope of her poetic works and traits and seeks to justify the stand of eminent critics like Sir Edmund Gosse, H.A.L. Fisher, James Darmesteter, Edward Thompson, Harihar Das and others that in matters of chronology and quality she is at the head of Indo-Anglian poets.

This work is the substantial part of my Ph.D. thesis. I would like to place on record my deep sense of gratitude to the university for permitting me to publish it and to the examiners for their avowal of it. I must also register my deep indebtedness to Dr. K.C. Bhatnagar, my supervisor and to Dr. A.N. Dwivedi, my *de facto* supervisor who guided my first steps in research and offered me valuable suggestions from time to time.

It would have been impossible for me to complete this work without the active co-operation of the staff of the National Library, Kolkata; Bombay University Library, Mumbai; Western Regional of Indian Council of Social Science Research, Mumbai; Delhi Public Library, Delhi; and Gurukula Kangri University Library, Hardwar. I extend my sincere thanks to the staff and the librarians of these centres of higher learning for their invaluable help to me.

I also feel a sense of obligation to many distinguished scholars for their timely assistance and wise counsel offered to me whenever I approached them. Those who deserve special mention include Dr. K.R.S. Iyengar, Prof. C.D. Narasimhaiah, Prof. Sisir Kumar Ghose, Dr. Prithwindranath Mukherjee, Dr. Sitansu Mitra, Dr. M.K. Naik and Mr. Dipendranth Mitra. Last but not least, I express my thanks to Swami Siddhananda of Najibabad (U.P.) for his constant encouragement.

The book will prove useful to the students and teachers of Indian English poetry and researchers in this field.

K.A. Agrawal

Contents

The Dawn of Indian English Literature

1

Toru Dutt (1856-77) occupies a prominent place in the history of Indo-Anglian poetry. When she started writing, Indo-Anglian poetry was in its infancy. Though mocked by destiny at every step, she went on with her work with firm determination and produced astounding results. Her predecessors like Derozio, Kasiprasad and Madhusudan were mere explorers in the field and it is not till we come to her that we find "the first solid achievement"[1] in Indo-Anglian poetry. The present study is intended to make an overall assessment of Toru Dutt's poetic achievement for which she is so well remembered today and will continue to be remembered even in the days to come.

In the early nineteenth century, there set in a movement in this country towards a new life and a new thought that is generally characterised as the Renaissance in India. This Renaissance, this new birth in India, became, in due course of time, a thing of immense importance both to herself and to the world—to herself because of all that is meant for her in the recovery or the change of her time-old spirit and national ideals, to the world because of the immense possibilities involved in the reasserting of a force that is in many respects unlike any other and its genius very different from the mentality and spirit that have hitherto governed the modern idea in mankind. Subtle critics and thinkers like James H. Cousins and Sri Aurobindo have touched suggestively various sides of the Renaissance in India.

The term 'Renaissance' carries the mind back to the turning-point of European culture to which it was first applied; that was not so much a reawakening as an overturn and reversal, a seizure of Christianised, Teutonised, feudalised

Europe by the old Graeco-Latin spirit and form with all the complex and momentous results which came from it. That is decidedly not a type of renaissance that is at all possible in India. There is a closer resemblance to the Celtic movement in Ireland, the attempt of a reawakened national spirit to find a new impulse of self-expression which shall give the spiritual force for a great reshaping and rebuilding: in Ireland this was discovered by a return to the Celtic spirit and culture after a long period of eclipsing English influences and in India something of the same kind of movement appeared and took a pronounced turn.

Cousins puts the question in his book, *The Renaissance in India* (1918), whether the word 'renaissance' at all applies in the Indian context since India has always been awake and stood in no need of reawakening. There is a certain truth in it and to one of open mind, struck by the living continuity of past and present India, it may be especially apparent; but that is not how we, the Indians see it. There was, beyond doubt, a period, brief but very disastrous, of the dwindling of that great fire of life, even a moment of incipient disintegration, an adventure by chance, inwardly by an increasing torpor of the creative spirit in religion and art (science and philosophy and intellectual knowledge being long dead or petrified into a mere scholastic punditism). All this pointed to a nadir of setting energy, the evening-time from which, according to the Indian concept of *yugas* (cycles of time), a new age had to start. It was that moment and the pressure of a superimposed European culture which followed it that made the reawakening inevitable.

Sri Aurobindo, while considering the question of the Renaissance in India, takes three factors into account: (i) the great past of Indian culture and life with the moment of inadaptive torpor into which it had lapsed, (ii) the first period of the Western contact in which it seemed for a moment likely to perish by slow decomposition, and (iii) the ascending movement which first broke some clarity of expression.[2] Cousins has fixed his eye on Indian spirituality which has always maintained itself even in the decline of the national vitality and which has always saved India at every critical moment of her destiny. It was certainly her spirituality which has been starting-point of her renaissance. Any other nation under the same pressure would have long ago perished soul and body. But India kept her essential spirit, though a great change overtook the body. The shaping of a new body, of new philosophical, artistic, literary, cultural, political, and social forms by the same soul rejuvenescent was the type of the Indian renaissance—forms not contradictory of the truths of life which the old expressed, but rather expressive of those truths restated, cured of defect, completed.[3]

British Rule in India

As a result of the Indian renaissance, nationalism along with spiritual forces began to assert itself. It sharply reacted against the imperialistic powers, especially the British regime. When the brave Britishers came to India, the Mughals were still in the saddle. In coming over to India, their basic design was to trade and 'get rich quick'. They succeeded in the pursuance of their design and established the East India Company in 1600 A.D. Taking advantage of the disturbing situations in the country, they grew ambitious and won many estates and became rulers here. They continued to govern the country uptil 1947 when the Indian people compelled them to quit and go.

The Beginnings of Education

While administering the country, the Englishmen gave attention to the problem of education. The burning question before them was whether India was to wholly Westernised system of education with English as the medium of instruction or she was merely to continue the study of Sanskrit and Persian and impart education with the various regional languages as media. Macaulay's celebrated "Minute" (of which we shall speak more a little later) clinched the issue at last in favour of English.

Although the East India Company was founded long ago, the Britishers cared little or nothing for the education of the Indian people up to the eighteenth century. Thereafter, the Governors of the provinces and successive Governor-General showed little interest in Hindu or Islamic culture and hence they did not tackle boldly the problem of illiteracy among the Indian masses. There were, at that time, four types of indigenous educational institutions in India:

1. Pathshalas of the Hindus;
2. Madrassas of the Muslims;
3. Persian Schools; and
4. Schools teaching through the modern Indian languages.[4]

Warren Hastings, no doubt, founded and liberally endowed the Calcutta Madrassa in 1781. In the previous year, James Augustus Hicky had brought out at Calcutta the first newspaper of the country, *Hicky's Bengal Gazette.*

Sir William Jones

It was actually Sir William Jones who showed a real interest in the education of India and his researches in the educational field ushered the country in a new era. He was a liberal Englishman and tried to understand the Indian populace and its problems. He had respects for the sacred literature of India and looked upon himself as a servant, rather than as a ruler, of the people in whose midst he had to live and move. In his poem, "Ode in Imitation of A lcaeus", he pointed out that not 'high-raised battlement, or laboured mound' constitutes a state; 'starred and spangled courts' are but dens 'where low-crowned baseness wafts perfumes to pride'; in his opinion, 'high-minded Men' alone make a strong and stable state. Jones founded the Royal Asiatic Society of Bengal and published powerful renderings of *Shakuntalam* and *Hitopadesha.* He addressed a number of odes to Hindu Gods and wrote a long verse tale. *The Enchanted Fruit*, which is based on the *Mahabharata* episode. Jones was an enlightened Englishman, who was a source of inspiration not only to his own countrymen, but also to Indians. He prompted them "to study the sacred Indian Literature reverently, to bring it to the notice of the masses, and to help the Indian renaissance to its fruitful blossoming in the fullness of time."[5] Jones and his comrades in Oriental scholarship were surely inspired by a stern, missionary zeal.

In 1791, Jonathan Duncan started the Sanskrit College at Banaras. Still India drifted for some fifty years more; neither Charles Grant's "Observations", nor Lord Moira's "Minute", nor the British Parliament's initiative in 1813, nor yet the formation of the Committee of Public Instruction in 1823, attempted any far-reaching solution of the educational problem.

In the meantime, three factors suddenly emerged and defined with great clarity the course of education in India for the next one hundred years and more. These were:

1. the new intellectualism and renascent ardour among the Indians, as symbolised by Raja Rammohan Roy;
2. the perseverance of the Christian missionaries; and above all,
3. the persuasiveness and metallic clarity of Macaulay's English prose style.[6]

Rammohan Roy and the Reformers

A select band of Indians headed by Raja Rammohan Roy had tasted the fruits of Western literature and culture at close quarters and they naturally contrasted the West at its best with the decadence of Indian civilisation. They were seized by a spirit of intolerance and aggressive reform. They strongly pleaded for the introduction of a system of Western education with English as the medium of instruction. With the generous help of two Englishmen, David Hare and Edward Hyde East, Raja Rammohan Roy inaugurated the Calcutta Hindu College, which later developed into Presidency College. Starting with only one hundred students in 1817, the college steadily grew much and more popular and the number of students quadrupled within the next twenty years. In Bombay and Madras, however, people were rather slow to follow Calcutta's lead in educational matters.

The renaissance in modern Indian literature begins with Raja Rammohan Roy. Born in a village (Radhanagore) in Bengal on May 22, 1772, he died at Bristol on September 27, 1833. Roy was destined to act as a bridge between India and England. He had mastered many languages—Sanskrit, Persian,

Arabic, Hindustani and Bengali. After travelling within and outside India and making some business ventures at Calcutta, he served in the districts under two British officials—Woodforde and Digby. While working with Digby, Roy completed his mastery of the English language. Resigning from the company service at last, Roy returned to Calcutta in 1814, started the Atriya Sabha and so launched himself on the consciousness of the Calcutta society. The next few years saw him in hectic activity. The plight of widows, the darkness of superstition, the miasma of ignorance, the general backwardness of the country, all stirred him to action. Though attracted by Christianity, Roy realised with sorrow that the bigoted Christian was as conceited as the bigoted Hindu. In 1821, he started a weekly paper, *Sambad Kaumudi,* which launched a sustained onslaught on the forces of prejudice and reaction. By 1823, he had fully matured, tested his friends and re-considered his ends and means. During the remaining ten years of his life, 1823-33, he crammed, in Brajendranath Seal's words, 'the work of half a dozen giants'. He was an intensely religious man, a Hindu and a Brahmin, who was always ready to accept 'the best' of Christianity and Islam. His name is permanently associated with the abolition of *sati* system (the forced burning of widows after the death of their husbands) and child-marriage. He was the founder of the Brahma Samaj.

Rammohan Roy published a number of pioneering works. In 1820, his *Precepts of Jesus, the Guide to Peace and Happiness* came out. It proves his intense respect for the gospels of Christianity. His other writings were: *Brief Remarks regarding Modern Encroachments on the Ancient Rights of Females according to the Hindu Law of Inheritance* (1822) and *Exposition of the Practical Operation of the Judicial and Revenue Systems of India, and of the General Character and Condition of its Native Inhabitants* (1832). Besides these brochures, he published several other papers and pamphlets touching upon almost every aspect of national life. He was indefatigable and refused to spare himself.

Besides Raja Rammohan Roy, there were many other reformers working at the same time. Among the members of the Brahma Samaj, there were Devendranath Tagore, Keshab Chandra Sen and others. Inspired by Roy, Keshab, in 1870, founded the "Indian Reform Association", which launched a comprehensive programme of social and educational reforms. The programme of the association was carried through five sections, each with a Secretary of its own. These sections were: (1) Female improvement, (2) Education of the working classes, (3) Cheap literature, (4) Temperance, and (5) Charity.[7]

The Brahma Samaj inspired similar other movements in India. The most important ones were the Prarthana Samaj and the Arya Samaj. The Prarthana Samaj was founded in 1867 in Bombay, its leader being Dr. Atmaram Pandurang (1823-98). Keshab Chandra Sen greatly influenced this Samaj; later, R.G. Bhandarkar and M.G. Ranade joined it and infused new strength in worship and social reform. It did not produce any new philosophy and literature, nor much missionary activity.[8] Broadly speaking, this Samaj subscribed to the beliefs of the Brahma Samaj.

The Arya Samaj was a more potential force in cultural and social fields than the Prarthana Samaj. It was founded by Swami Dayananda Saraswati in 1875 in Bombay. The Arya Samaj laid down some fundamental doctrines and rules of conduct. Three of these may be noted here:

1. The (Arya) Samaj shall regard the *Vedas* alone as independently and absolutely authoritative.
2. Every member shall cheerfully contribute a hundredth part of the money he has earned towards the fund of the Samaj, the Arya Vidyalaya and the *Arya Prakash* paper.
3. The *Vedas* and ancient *Arsha Granthas* shall be studied and taught in the Arya Vidyalaya and true and right training, calculated to improve males and females, shall be imparted on Vedic lines.

In 1877, these doctrines were replaced by the Ten Principles. Instead of No. 1 above, it simply laid down that the *Vedas* are the Books of True Knowledge which the members should study. The other nine principles merely inculcated virtue and morality to which no religion can possibly take any exception. The most characteristic feature of the Arya Samaj is the emphasis it laid upon the work of *Shuddhi*. This means the reconversions of those Hindus—millions in number—who had once been willingly or unwillingly converted into other religions like Islam or Christianity, but were now willing to come back to the fold of Hinduism. Orthodox Hinduism had always barred its door against them; the Arya Samaj threw it wide open. Two other distinctive features of the Samaj are social services like famine-relief and the spread of English education. The Dayananda Anglo-Vedic School at Lahore soon developed into a college and has become the pattern of many educational institutions maintained by the Samaj. The curriculum in these colleges was not exactly in the original spirit of Dayananda and so the more orthodox section founded the Gurukul at Hardwar. It is "a unique institution to perpetuate the educational ideals of ancient India".[9]

Apart from these Samajas and their distinguished followers, the names of Ramakrishna Paramahansa and Swami Vivekananda will always be remembered for their contributions to the furtherance of the cause of social and spiritual regeneration of the country. They were great saints and seers and had realised God. They strove to reveal "the harmony of all religions".[10] The reputation earned by Swami Vivekananda through the Parliament of Religions at Chicago (U.S.A.) made him a world figure and raised the prestige of India and Hinduism very high. He laid the foundation of the great organisation—Ramakrishna Math and Mission—which bears the name of his *guru*. It was he who made it "the greatest spiritual force in modern India".[11]

The Missionaries

The second factor which determined the course of education in India was the advent and activities of Christian missionaries. The ultimate aim of the missionaries has always been the proselytisation of the Hindu, Muslim and other non-Christian communities in India. They did some pioneering work in the field of education and social service. The earliest among them were the three protestant missionaries—Carey, Marshman and Ward who began their work at the Danish Settlement of Serampore in 1793. They have become famous in history as the *Serampore Trio* and it must be admitted that they made an excellent combination from the missionary point of view because Carey was a great propagandist, Ward was a painter and Marshman a school teacher. But their zeal outran among Indians by their publication entitled *Addresses to Hindus and Mahomedans.* The Company had to intervene and reaffirm its policy of religious neutrality. The missionaries and their friends began an agitation in England intended to show that the anti-missionary policy of the Company was opposed to the teachings of Christ and that its neglect of the education of the Indian people was absolutely unjustifiable. Their agitation obtained considerable support in Charles Grant (1746-1823) and led ultimately to the educational clause of the Charter Act of 1813. Side by side with this agitation in England, some of the Company's officials in India supported the cause of Indian education. Prominent among them was Lord Minto, who was the Governor-General of India during 1806-13. Minto was personally an admirer of Oriental literature and felt that its study would be useful to the Western nations themselves. He was, therefore, very anxious that Englishman should give all possible encouragement to the study and preservation of Indian culture. In a Minute, dated 6th March 1811, he wrote:

> It is seriously to be lamented that a nation particularly distinguished for its love and successful cultivation of letters in other parts of the empire should have failed to extend its fostering care to the literature of the Hindoos, and to aid in opening to the learned in Europe the repositories of their literature.[12]

As a result of this combined agitation in England and India the question of Indian education came up for discussion when the Charter of the Company became due for renewal in 1813. The subject that was discussed most was that of a suitable agency for the spread of Indian education. One party, whose view is typified in that of Charles Grant, believed that the best education for Indians was to teach them English through the missionaries. The other party, which was represented by Minto, believed that the best education for Indians was that of their own classics through the liberal endowment from the Company. The Charter Act of 1813 reconciled the views of both parties and proved a turning-point in the history of Indian education. With it, agitation which Grant and Wilberforce carried on for nearly twenty years came to successful conclusion; the education of the Indian people was now included within the duties of the Company; a comparatively large amount was annually fixed for acquisition of land in India and establishment of English schools, thereby laying the foundation of the modern educational system.

The period of twenty years between that two great Charters of the Company, viz. those of 1813 and 1838, was one of the experiments in the field of Indian education. The Charter of 1838 made the provisions that no Indian should be debarred from holding any post under the Company by reason of his caste or creed. It also threw India open to missionaries from all countries.

Lord Macaulay and After

The third factor to decide the course of education in India was Lord Macaulay's "Minute", dated 2nd February 1835, which is a document of great historical significance. Macaulay was of the view that it was necessary and possible to make natives of this country good English scholars and that to this end our efforts ought to be directed. About the medium of instruction on grounds of expediency and desirability, Macaulay observed thus:

> All parties seem to be agreed on one point, that the dialects commonly spoken among the natives of this part of India contain neither literary nor scientific information, and are moreover too poor and crude that, until they are enriched from some other quarter, it will not be easy to translate any valuable work into them. It seems to be admitted on all sides that the intellectual improvement of those classes of

> the people who have the means of pursuing higher studies can at present be effected only by means of some language not vernacular amongst them.[13]

This condemnation of the spoken language of the people naturally left the choice of a medium of instruction between Sanskrit and Arabic on the one hand and English on the other. Macaulay admittedly did not know either Arabic or Sanskrit, but he gave it as the considered opinion that 'a single shelf of a good European library was worth the whole native literature of India and Arabia'. On the other hand, Macaulay was eloquent in praise of English and its utility in India because of its being the language of the ruling class, the language of commerce throughout the East and because of the familiarity already gained with it by the higher classes of Indians. Macaulay strongly recommended that the object of educational policy in India should be the spread of Western learning through the medium of the English language. He also suggested that the existing institutions of oriental learning should be closed forthwith and that funds thus released should be used for the promotion of English education.

On March 7, 1835, the Governor-General-in-Council accorded official sanction to Macaulay's policy. Lord William Bentinck passed the Resolution that "the great object of the British Government ought to be the promotion of European literature and science among the natives of India; and that all the funds appropriated for the purpose of education would be best employed on English education alone".[14]

But the matter did not end with the adoption of Lord Bentinck's resolution. There was a conflict brewing between the Indian languages on the one hand and English on the other. To close this conflict, Lord Auckland, the then Governor-General of India, put forth his formula of compromise, which is usually known as "Auckland's Minute". Lord Auckland shrewdly guessed that the real cause of the conflict was financial and that each party—Oriental and Anglican—would allow the other to work undisturbed if adequate funds were made available for both. The entire additional cost was estimated at Rs. 31,000 per annum and Lord Auckland gladly accepted it to satisfy the Oriental party without harming the interests of the Anglicists. However, the medium of instruction continued to be English as suggested by Macaulay. Lord Auckland turned down the recommendations of Adam regarding the improvement and extension of indigenous elementary schools. He considered Adam's plan as "utopian and impracticable", but had he accepted it, the history of mass education in India would have been different.

Of great historical significance was Wood's Despatch of July 19, 1854, also known as *The Education Despatch of the Court of Directors*. Charles Wood was then the President of the Board of Control. The despatch was a long document of a hundred paragraphs and deals with several questions of great educational importance. It mentions the objects of educational policy pursued by the Company, the controversy between the Anglicists and the Company, the controversy between the Anglicists and the Orientalists and the medium of instruction. It directs that English and Indian language should be cultivated *together* to spread proper education in India. It also spells out certain new schemes, such as the establishment of the Education Department in each of the five provinces, the setting up of Universities, the creation of a network of Graded Schools all over India, the increase in Grant-in-aid, the training of teachers, the employment of educated Indians and females education. Soon after the receipt of the Despatch of 1854, every provincial Government in India organised a Department of Public Instruction under a Director. An adequate number of educational inspectors were appointed in order to assist the Director in his work. Large sums of money were made available to the Education Departments for the execution of their schemes and the organisation of the modern system of education in India began in right earnest.

The above account of the beginnings of education in India informs us how English came to stay in this country. From it we also learn that the germs of Indo-Anglian literature may be discovered in the early days of English education in India.

Under the Macauleyan dispensation (which was the backbone of English education in India), education was to be imparted to the select few in the government institutions. But it was expected that the young men who thus received education would return to their villages and spread new education to the masses. Thus, from the intellectual classes culture was to filter down and in a decade or two the Utopia of mass education would be within sight. But these expectations proved altogether illusory. The educated Indians made efficient teachers and patient clerks: some fared remarkably well as administrators and judges. There were publicists and platform orators too. People had even begun to believe that the future of India was bright and the redemption was near.

But the 'filtration theory' did not work. The hungry sheep looked up and were not fed. And also, the newly educated Indian tended to be "an absurd copy of his Western contemporary".[15] The educated community evolved into a superior caste drifted apart and speedily lost touch with the masses. The alien culture learned at schools and colleges made Indian youths hanker after the thrills of urban life and finally made them "incredible anachronisms" in their own once happy homes. A new generation conversed and corresponded in English 'Indianisms' and 'Babuisms' were the order of the day. Under such circumstances, the wit of the educated Indian seesawed between his mother-tongue and English and again between the Western and Oriental civilisations. It was surely an uncongenial atmosphere which would hardly permit any healthy literary growth.

The Birth of Indo-Anglian Literature

Even then, many Indians quickly mastered the intricacies of the English language and made it a fit vehicle for the communication of ideas. Poetic composition was not yet possible, but letters, memoranda, monographs and translations in English appeared in due course. Presently, Indians boldly ventured into the domain of journalism; they published political and economic pamphlets, partial portraits of men of importance, even occasional skits and short stories. As more and more Indians received education in English, the Indo-Anglian found his audience increasing and this naturally encouraged him to write more frequently.

Another factor that inspired the Indo-Anglian to attempt self-expression in English was the meritorious work of the Anglo-Indian poets. Sir William Jones, John Leyden, Henry Derozio, Meredith Parker, David Lester Richardson, Sir Edwin Arnold, Sir Alfred Lyall, Trego Webb, Lawrence Hope and William Waterfield were among the many Anglo-Indian administrators and Orientalists who derived their poetic inspiration from traditional Indian themes and thus added a new chapter to the story of English poetry. Indians who read the works of these poets were in turn inspired to try their own hands at poetic composition. They had before them for their models the unique achievements of the Anglo-Indians and the great masters—Milton, Wordsworth, Shelley, Keats, Tennyson, etc.—of English literature, but spiritual sustenance was yet lacking. The Indo-Anglians of the early days were the creators of a civilisation arrested on the way; their past was a hazy thing of humiliations and frustrations and their future was an intriguing and uncertain thing. They were, thus, in a state of spiritual drift and rudderlessness. By and by, the clouds began to clear and out of life-giving rains of a new culture they tried to re-discover their souls. In this great of the re-discovery, Bengal took the lead and pulled the country out of stupor.

Some other Pioneers

The earliest writings of Indo-Anglians were, as noted earlier, in prose. The Indians of a century ago or so had to talk to or appeal to their English rulers on various subjects of public importance. A speech had to be carefully prepared; a pamphlet had to be written and published. As the number of English-knowing Indians increased, publications also got diversified. The prose writings of Raja Rammohan Roy have already been noted. Roy showed, through his pioneering books, a new direction to talented people with creative urge. Beside Rammohan Roy, there were many other Indian writers of prose in those days. Their works can be seen in old libraries of the country, although their intrinsic value is almost negligible.

Hassan Ali's *Observations on the Musalmans of India* (1832) is among the earliest books written by a Muslim on Muslims. P. Raja Gopaul's *Mission to Siam* (1820) and Mohan Lal's *Travels in the Punjab* (1834) are among the early of travel books or memoirs, Kavali Venkata Ramaswami's *Biographical Sketches of Dekkan Poets* embodies crude attempts at biography. In the realm of poetry, too, the earliest attempt by an Indian was made in 1830 when Kashiprasad Ghose's *The Shair and Other Poems* appeared. Thus, English seemingly came to stay and Indo-Anglian literature became a reality. The contributions of Bengal to the growth of Indo-Anglian literature have been immense and remarkable. The renaissance in India is mostly due to them.

NOTES

1. B.K. Talookdar, "The Poetry of Toru Dutt", *Journal of the University of Bombay,* VI, part 6 (May 1936), p. 71.
2. Sri Aurobindo, *The Renaissance in India* (Pondicherry: Sri Aurobindo Ashram Trust, 1973), p. 4.
3. *Ibid.*, pp. 4-5.
4. Syed Nurullah and J.P. Naik, *A Student's History of Education in India*: *1800-1947*, Rev. ed. (Bombay: Macmillan & Co. Ltd., 1949), p. 2.
5. K.R. Srivinivasa Iyengar, *The Indian Contribution to English Literature* (Bombay: Karnatak Publishing House, 1954), pp. 2-3.
6. *Ibid.*, p. 3.
7. R.C. Majumdar et al., *British Paramountcy and Indian Renaissance*, Part II (Bombay: Bhartiya Vidya Bhavan, 1965), p. 104.
8. *Ibid.*, p. 106.
9. *Ibid.*, p. 110.
10. *Ibid.*, p. 111.
11. *Ibid.*, 122.
12. Quoted from *A Student's History of Education*, pp. 48-49.
13. Quoted from *A Student's History of Education*, pp. 70-71.
14. *Ibid.*, p. 72.
15. K.R. Srinivasa Iyengar, *Indo-Anglian Literature* (Bombay: The International Book House Ltd., 1943), p. 6.

The Pioneers of Indian English Literature

2

In the 19th century, a number of promising writers adorned the galaxy of Indo-Anglian poetry and thereby enriched its stock and quickened the pace of its growth and expansion. The Ghoses and the Dutts and a few others gained for it 'a local habitation and a name'. Hereafter we shall make a survey of these distinguished writers one by one in order to ascertain their individual contributions to the development of Indian poetry in English.

Henry Louis Vivian Derozio

Henry Derozio's name comes on top among these writers. His father was a Portuguese gentleman and his mother an Indian lady. He was educated in the Dhurrumtolah Academy of David Drummond. He showed early signs of poetic talent. At the age of fourteen, Derozio entered the mercantile firm of Messrs James Scott & Co. soon he was transferred to Bhagalpur, where he suddenly discovered himself to be a poet. Intimacy with Nature possibly quickened his poetic sensibilities.

Derozio's early piece drew the attention of Dr. John Grant and others who then mattered in Calcutta. At eighteen, Derozio was offered a professorship in the Calcutta Hindu College, where he quickly gained the esteem and affection of his wards. He was one of the earliest teachers of English in the country, but, more than that, he was constant source of inspiration to his pupils. He made them read and think for themselves. His love for his students later found an excellent poetic expression in the lines:

Expanding like the petals of young flowers,
I watch the gentle opening of your minds,
And the sweet loosening of spell that binds,
Your intellectual energies and powers,
That stretch (like young birds in soft summer hours)
Their wings to try their strength. O! how the winds
Of circumstance, and freshening April showers
Of early knowledge, and unnumbered kinds
Of new perceptions, shed their influence,
And how you worship Truth's omnipotence!
What joyance rains upon me, when I see,
Fame in the mirror of futurity,
Weaving the chaplets you are yet to gain–
And then I feel I have not lived in vain.

But this relationship was too good to last long. Derozio was misunderstood by the public and he had to resign from his job. He then turned to journalism and began editing and publishing *The East Indian,* which did some notable work. At the age of twenty-two, Derozio died of cholera on December 23, 1831. In Mr. Oaten's words, "What English literature lost through the early death of Keats, Anglo Indian literature lost, in lesser degree, when Derozio died; for in both men there was a passionate temperament combined with unbounded sympathy with nature. Both died while their powers were not yet fully developed."

Derozio was a great lover of India. He had full knowledge of India's past. He apostrophises the country of his birth in these moving lines:

My country, in thy days of glory past
A beauteous halo circled round thy brow,
And worshipped as a deity thou wast,...
Where is that glory, where that reverence now?
The eagle pinion is chained down at last,
And grovelling in the lowly dust are thou;

The minstrel hath no wreath to wreathe for thee
Save the sad story of thy misery.
... ...
And let the guerdon of my labour be,
My fallen country, one kind word for thee.

Derozio totally identified himself with India and hence he has been rightly called the National Bard of Modern India. He was a true predecessor of the great Thakur Rabindranath Tagore. Derozio was not unconscious of his mission, for he said with commendable self-knowledge and humility:

Many a hand more worthy far than mine
Once thy harmonious chords to sweetness gave:
Those hands are cold, but if those notes divine
May be thy mortal wakened once again,
Harp of my country, let me strike the strain.

It is really sad that the country lost Derozio so soon.

As a poet, Derozio is mainly admired for the great promise he displayed in his published work. Like Keats and Chatterton before him, like Toru and Aru after him, Derozio moved in the field of poetry for a brief period; all of them were alike, in the Shelleyan phrase, 'inheritors of unfulfilled renown'. Derozio's sonnets and poems are "competent, sustained by deep feeling and executed with good craftsmanship; again and again, he achieved that fusion between thought and expression, feeling and form, which signifies all true poetry".[1]

But Derozio's technique is mostly derivative. He wrote under the spell of Byron and Thomas Moore. His work, *The Fakir of Jungheera and Other Poems,* is full of Byronic echoes. In it the Brahmin widow, Nuleeni, is beautifully delineated. She escapes *Sati* at the last moment being carried away by a robber-chief; but other sufferings now embrace her and she loses her robber chief. Thus, she becomes a widow twice. She clasps the dead body of the chief frantically.

as if she dreamed
Of him in her embrace: but they who thought
That life was tenanting her breast, and sought
Some answer from her heart to hush the doubt,
Found that its eloquence had all burned out.

Nuleeni finds her peace in the blissful union of death.

Derozio was courageous and fearless in his life. Even on his death-bed did not lose either his equanimity or his brave faith. Like Donne, Derozio faced the awful mystery of death challengingly.

But man's eternal energies can make
An atmosphere around him, and so take
Good out of evil, like the yellow bee
That sucks from flowers malignant a sweet treasure,
O tyrant fate! thus shall I vanquish thee,
For out of suffering shall I gather pleasure.

Derozio lived a fine life. He loved his pupils, his vocation and his country very well. He was brave unto his last. And when he expired, his body was emtombed in the South Park Street burial-ground in Calcutta.

The noble tradition established by Henry Derozio was continued by Captain David Lester Richardson. This famous teacher came to India as an ensign in the Bengal Infantry. In 1824, ill-health forced him to return to England, where he started writing. When he came back to India in 1829, he became the editor of *The Calcutta Literary Gazette* and *The Bengal Annual.* Later on, he was appointed *aide-de-camp* to Lord William Bentinck and in 1836 he became, through the influence of Lord Macaulay, the Principal of the Hindu College and for the next twenty-five years he was devoted to the teaching of English literature, language and history. His *Selection from the British Poets,* published in 1840 at the suggestion of Macaulay, shows his liberal view of the range of literature. His poems and essays offer us a delightful reading. He took delight in the art of interpretation. He was a very good reader of English verse, especially that of Shakespeare.

The patrons of the Hindu College were as remarkable as the teachers there. There are frequent references in contemporary notes and letters to the quaint figure of David Hare, with long blue coat adorned with large brass buttons, moving in and out of the classrooms or attending the debates of the Academic Association. Mr. Hare's role as a patron of education in Calcutta cannot be, in any way, minimised.

Kashiprasad Ghose (1809-73)

Bengalis were also not lagging behind in the job of writing good English poetry. Taught by men who themselves were poets, they attempted to demonstrate their mastery of the new language and literature. The first Bengali publication in English verse belongs to the year 1830 when Kashiprasad Ghose wrote his well-known *The Shair and Other Poems*. It was a book of about 200 pages, printed by the India Gazette Press and dedicated to Lord William Bentinck. The influence of Sir Walter Scott is apparent in this book. Its various cantos are separately dedicated to such famous contemporaries as Horace Hayman Wilson and Henry Meredith Parker. Ghose successfully captured it the tone and spirit of Scott's *The Lay of the Last Minstrel*. His work shows traces of his readings in the minor love poets of the Romantic school. Here is a piece of good imitative writing.

> I would I were the zephyr sweet,
> To kiss thy face and round it play;
> And when thou sigh'st for love, to greet
> Those sighs, and steal their sweets away,
> I would I were the witnesses pure,
> That clings unto thy bosom's swell;
> That others I'd to madness line,
> While I myself there safely dwell.

Ghose's book contains several poems on Indian festivals after the manner of Sir William Jones' hymns to the Hindu deities. The verse is "agreeably imitative and everywhere pleasing".[2] There is little originality either in the form of the poems or in their themes. However, Richardson's delightful anthology of prose and poetry, *The Bengal Annal*, published on seven occasions between 1833 and 1836 contains some pieces of Ghose. This is sufficient proof that in his own day the Bengali poet had earned reputation as a writer of English verse.

Rajnarain Dutt

Many young writers of the day looked to Richardson for encouragement and patronage. Such one was Rajnarain Dutt, who dedicated his work to Richardson. Rajnarain Dutt wrote *Osmyn, an Arabian Tale* (1841), a lengthy poem in heroic couplets. This poem is partly pleasingly reminiscent of an antique manner of presentation:

> What thundering sound upon the midnight wind
> Comes louder and yet louder from behind?
> The caverned echoes wake; the vaults of stone
> Relieve the chattering tramp in varied tone
> Who comes so late and armed, at deadlong speed;
> With sable turbon, cloak and barbed steed?

It is actually nothing short of a lengthy experiment in pentameters.

Michael Madhusudan Dutt (1824-73)

It was left to Michael Madhusudan Dutt to write something substantial and lasting. Born in 1824 and educated in the Hindu College, he was the favourite pupil of Richardson, who encouraged him to authorship. Madhusudan Dutt accepted Christianity and migrated to Madras in search of a job and edited for some time an English newspaper in that metropolis. He married a European lady, qualified for the bar in England and tried to make a living as a lawyer. He led a chequered career and died in the prime of his life and at the height of his powers in a Calcutta hospital. His long metrical romance in English was *The Captive Ladie*, an attempt to tell the story of

Prithvi Raj, the Rajput King of Delhi. It was published in 1849 and won at once the hearts of literary people. Madhusdan's other works in English include *Visions of the Past* in blank verse, *Ratnavali* (1858), translations of *Sarmista* (1859) and the farce, *Is This Called Civilization*? (1871).

During the latter part of his life, Madhusudan wrote mainly in Bengali and his fame solely rests on the Bengali epic, *Meghnad-Badha*, of which an English rendering was published in 1879.

Madhusudan inspired many young poets to write. In his "In Memoriam", the poet Nabokissen Ghose (Ram Sharma) wrote as follows:

> Hushed is the tuneful voice that thrilled the soul,
> Silent the lyre whose swelling notes did roll
> In streams of music sweet that did impart
> A life—a soul even to the dullest heart!

And Sri Aurobindo also paid tributes to the poet. In his moving commemoration ode he wrote:

> No human hands such notes ambrosial moved;
> These accents are not of the imperfect earth;
> Rather, the god was voiceful in their birth,
> The god himself of the enchanting flute,
> The god himself took up thy pen and wrote.

The Dutt Family

Even during the days of Madhusudan, the Dutt family had distinguished itself for its literary and creative activities in the whole of Bengal. In the year 1851, Hur Chunder Dutt produced in Calcutta a small volume of poetry called *Fugitive Pieces*, many of which were reprinted twenty years later in his second volume entitled *Lotus Leaves*. Both works are slight, but they contain a pleasing variety of themes drawn from Indian history. *The Dutt Family Album* (1870) containing about 200 poems was written by Govin Chunder Dutt, Omesh Chunder

Dutt, Greece Chunder Dutt and Hur Chunder Dutt, three of whom were the sons of Rasamoy Dutt, the Secretary of the Hindu College Committee and a Commissioner of the Court of Requests. The volume was published in London by Messrs Longmans, Green & Co. For a student of Bengali literature, it is a work of great interest and importance. In the preface, the joint authors declare it to be the piece of 'a curiosity' and one of 'foreigners, natives of India...educated out of India'. In fact, this *Album* is the first to 'represent the older school of Bengali poetry, in English'. It was actually the compilation of men who received inspiration from Captain Richardson and whose academic career began and ended in the Hindu College. The literary merits of the work, judged in the light of the special circumstances of its production, are considerable. The quality of the verse, the range and variety of theme, the command of various metrical forms and the restraint and dignity of the style are everywhere pleasing. The most notable of the four writers were Govin Chunder Dutt and Omesh Chunder Dutt, who produced 66 and 73 poems respectively out of a total of 197. Indian history, legend and landscape, the picturesque elements of the Christian and the Hindu faith and such ideas as would attract an Oriental in his first inter-course with the West, provide the subjects of their poems.

Govin Chunder Dutt

The contributions made by Govin Chunder to the *Album* were primarily of a didactic character. More than any of his collaborators, Govin was touched by Christian sentiment, and found his themes either in the Christian theology or in narratives from the scriptures. He had a wonderful command of an intricate stanza-form when he wrote on the subject of Wordsworth's poetry and concluded as follows:

> Hail, ye Rydalian laurels that have grown
> Untended by the poet's calm abode,
> And in the foot-paths that he ever trod.

Wrapt in deep thought, at evening time, alone;
... ...
A crown of amaranth by her own hands made.

The *Album* throws light on the atmosphere of Govin's house, an ideal atmosphere by all means for Aru Dutt and Toru Dutt.

Omesh Chunder Dutt

Omesh Chunder Dutt was attracted mainly by the stirring incidents of Indian legend. He wrote with ease and contributed the largest number of poems to the *Album*. He provided much interesting verse for such periodicals as Mukerjee's *Magazine*. It is unfortunate that his "undoubted talent for narrative did not find greater scope in the abundant historical material of India".[3] He might have written a fine body of heroic verse, had he continued such studies in Tod's *Annals of Rajasthan* as inspired his vigorous poem, "The Chief of Pokurna." One may mark the beauty and the power of description in the following stanza of this poem:

Oh! gaily in a golden shower
The setting sun-light falls,
Upon the waste of glinting sand
which girds Pokurna's walls.

The poet had a wonderful faculty of observation and could describe natural scenes and sights with great charm and command.

The other collaborators of *The Dutt Family Album* were Greece Chunder Dutt and Hur Chunder Dutt. The latter has already been examined, and his part in the *Album* was slight and amounted to eleven poems in all.

Greece Chunder Dutt

Greece Chunder Dutt contributed 47 pieces to the *Album*. In 1887, he published a separate volume of poems entitled *Cherry Blossoms*. In this volume several earlier contributions to the *Album* were reprinted, but the greater number of poems were fresh. The volume was carefully produced and contained much that was of value and attraction. The author had specialised in the difficult sonnet form. The subjects of these poems are as varied as India. The solemnity of the sonnets is relieved by the more lively measures of the historical and legendary poems. At times one comes across heroic stanzas in the volume that might delight the heart of school-boy, such as the "Samarsi".

> Samarsi the bold is the pride of his clan,
> But he owns not an acre in broad Rajasthan;
> ... ...
> And Samarsi the bold is an exile from home.

With this volume of Greece Chunder, the poetical efforts of the gifted quarter of relatives may be said to have reached the highest peak of achievement.

Aru Dutt and Toru Dutt were fortunate enough to have been born in the renowned Dutt family at Rambagan (Calcutta). They were the worthy daughters of Govin Chunder, a poet and linguist of fame and Kshetramoni, a gentle lady of refined sensibility. Besides contributing to the *Album* (as noted above), Govin had also published *The Loyal Hours* (1876) and *Cherry Stones* (1881), both containing good English verses. Mrs. Govin was well-versed in English and Bengali. She was mainly responsible in giving a fine taste to her daughters in literary performance. She had translated *The Blood of Jesus into Bengali.* Born and bred in such a cultured family, it was natural for Aru and Toru to take up serious literary activities.

Aru Dutt

Aru (1854-74) translated only eight poems from French for inclusion in *A Sheaf Gleaned in French Fields*, which is largely the work of her younger sister, Toru Dutt. Thus, Toru has done no independent work. But she was a very good painter. She died of consumption at the age of twenty. On her death Toru wrote to her Cambridge friend, Miss Mary Martin in the following manner: "The Lord has taken dear Aru from us. It is a sore trial for us, but His will be done. We know he dooth all things for our good...."[4]

NOTES

1. K.R.S. Iyengar, *Indian Contribution to English Literature,* p. 12.
2. T.O.D. Dunn, *The Bengal Book of English Verse* (Bombay: Longmans, 1918), p. 5.
3. Dunn, *op. cit.*, p. 11.
4. Harihar Das, *The Life and Letters of Toru Dutt* (London: Oxford Univ. Press, 1921), p. 65.

Contribution of Dutt-Family to Indian English Literature

3

Aru's younger sister, Toru Dut, too, prematurely passed away. The life of Toru Dutt is a mixed story of sunshine and sorrow, beauty and tragedy, success and repentance. If her literary works fill us with wonder and delight, her early death leaves us sad and repenting.

Her Life

Born in a Hindu family on March 4, 1856, Toru Dutt was brought up by her parents with all care and affection. She had a rich and respectable ancestry. Attracted by the glamour of the West, the Dutts accepted Christianity. Then Toru was six, Aru was eight and their brother Abju was eleven. The conversion of faith caused a temporary estrangement between the parents, as may be inferred from Govin's poem addressed to his wife:

> Nay part not so—one moment stay,
>   Repel me not with scorn,
> Like others, wilt thou turn away,
>   And leave me quite forlorn?
> Wilt thou too join the scoffing crowd.
> The cold, the heartless, and the proud,
>   Who curse the hallowed worn,
> When, daring idols to disown,
>   I knelt before the Saviour's throne?

Mrs. Govin, however, seems to have reconciled herself to the changed situation and indeed to have become "an ardent Christian".[1]

Toru was frail and fragile in her physical appearance. When she was a little girl, her father wrote of her as follows:

> Puny and elf-like, with dishevelled tresses,
> Self-willed and shy—ne'er heeding that I call,
> Intent to pay her tenderest addresses
> To bird or cat,—but most intelligent...

He also wrote of his loving son thus:

> Most loving is my eldest, and I love him most;
> Almost a man in seeming, yet a child...

And thus of Aru:

> My next, the beauty of our home is meek,
> Not so deep-loving haply, but less wild
> Then her dear brother;—brow and blushing cheek
> Her nature shows serene, and pure, and mild
> As evening's early star...

The children had a private tutor, but Govin himself took a hand in their education. The first calamity that befell the family was the death of Abju at the age of 14, in 1865. For their consolation, the sisters began to read *Paradise Lost* repeatedly till it became a part of their poetic make-up. This is responsible for Toru's poetry abounding in "fair phrase and sonority".[2] She had also read Shakespeare well.

In 1869, the Dutt family left for Europe and the two girls attended a French school at Nice. A year later, the family went to London, where Toru and Aru took lessons in music and became "good musicians".[3] Living in a furnished house here, they started translation into English. Their cousin, Romesh Chander Dutt, was then in London, preparing for the Civil Services examinations. He used to call on them every now and then and remove their loneliness. Toru's knowledge of French and English was "astonishing".[4] So intimately did she identify herself with everything that was French that French became her favourite language and France the country of her choice. In the words of Sir Edmund Gosse, "To the end of her days Toru was a better French than English scholar. She loved French best, she knew its literature best, she wrote its language with more perfect elegance."[5]

In 1871, the Dutt family moved to Cambridge where both the sisters attended the lecturers for women and made friends with Miss Mary Martin, who was to be Toru's lifelong friend and the recipient of most of her letters.

In 1873, the entire family returned to Calcutta after a lapse of four years. Now the sisters plunged into "a feverish dream of intellectual effort and imaginative production".[6] They also divided their time between the city-house at Rambagan and the garden-house at Baugmaree. But the literary strain sustained by Aru proved to be fatal for her and she, aged 20, succumbed to consumption. It was a heart-rending calamity for Toru and Govin Chunder.

Toru along with her father started studying Sanskrit in 1875. She now made arrangement for the publication of *A Sheaf Gleaned in French Fields*, which appeared in 1876. In the meantime, she began hoping to 'bring out another *Sheaf*, not gleaned in French but in Sanskrit Fields'. The following extracts from her letters to Mary tell an inspiring tale about the circumstances in which she undertook her studies in Sanskrit and about the courses therein:

1. I have now nothing to do, so Papa and I are going to take up Sanskrit. It is a difficult language, and it is hard to learn it properly in less than 6 or 7 years, but I will try my best. My grandfather, Papa's father, used to know and understand Sanskrit like a pundit; and he only learnt it two or three years when he was forty-two or forty-three of age; so I hope, my case will not be holeless.[7]
2. We have begun Sanskrit: the pundit is very pleased with our eagerness to learn, and hopes great things from our assiduity. It is a very difficult language, as I said before, especially the grammar, which is dreadful.

It is not so difficult to read and understand it, for one who knows Bengali.[8]

3. We are going on with our Sanskrit lessons. When we have finished the book we are reading now, we shall take up Valmiki's *Ramayana*.[9]
4. The Sanskrit is going on tolerably well; we are now reading the *Ramayana*.[10]
5. Our Sanskrit is going on but slowly. We are now reading extracts from the *Mahabharata*.[11]
6. We are now reading *Sakuntala* in Sanskrit.[12]
7. I am translating some small Sanskrit pieces.[13]
8. I hope I shall be able to bring out another, 'sheaf', not gleaned in French but in Sanskrit Fields;... I have only as yet gathered two ears....[14]

From these extracts we infer that within a space of barely ten months Toru Dutt learnt Sanskrit, laved in the *Ramayana*, the *Mahabharata* and *Sakuntala* and translated a few pieces from the original Sanskrit into English verse. Toru was also well-read in the *Vishnu Purana* and the *Bhagavad Gita*. These readings gave 'her woman's imagination free play'.[15]

By 1877, Toru's health had run down; she was ill, very ill, and had recurrent attacks of fever, cough spasm and blood-spitting. She was obliged to keep within doors and was so weak that she could not even write her letters. It is a harrowing tale indeed. On August 30, 1877, Toru breathed her last, leaving behind her parents totally deserted and depressed. Govin reported peaceful death of his dear daughter to Mary Martin as follows: "Her end here was very peaceful and happy, and her mother and myself will never, never forget the expression that was on her face when all was over. Such a glory there was on it."[16] Toru was buried at the C.M.S. Cemetery in Calcutta, near her loved brother and sister.

Her Work

Toru appeared in print for the first time in December 1874, when her first essay secured in *The Bengal Magazine*. The same magazine brought out one more essay by Toru Dutt in the same

December number. One of these essays was on Leconte de Lisle and the other on Henry Vivian Derozio. Both essays were of a good length.

In June and July 1875, appeared *A Scene from Contemporary History*, which contained two translations in prose made by Toru Dutt from two speeches delivered, not long ago, in the French Legislative Assembly. One of these speeches was by Victor Hugo in which he, in 1851, vehemently opposed the proposal to bring about certain constitutional changes designed to make Louis Napoleon the virtual king of France and the other was delivered by M. Theirs, in 1870, strongly objecting to the proposal of declaring war by France on the king of Prussia. Toru's "unique linguistic abilities"[17] are evidenced in these translations. In several passages she aptly expressed, with freedom of language, the thought of the speaker. She fails, however, to do so uniformly and some of her renderings are not as happy or suitable as they should have been. But this can be realised only by a very scrupulous reader.

On November 23, 1875, Toru informed her British friend, "I have finished my book of French poetry translated into English."[18] The manuscript was then shown to a number of publishing firms, but 'Calcutta publishers were', according to Toru, 'a very timid class of people, not at all enterprising and they are besides more given to the sale of books than publishing new ones'. And so, it was to be printed only and not published, in 1876, under the title *A Sheaf Gleaned in French Fields* (more details about it will follow in the next chapter).

A Sheaf was the only volume that Toru saw through the press in her life. After her death, her father examined her papers and found, among other things, an unfinished romance in English, entitled *Bianca,* or *The Young Spanish Maiden* and a complete French novel called *Le Journal de Mademoiselle d' Arvers*.

Bianca was published serially in *The Bengal Magazine* between January and April 1878. The circumstances of the heroine of this unfinished tale, Bianca Garcia, the younger and only surviving daughter of a Spanish gentleman who had settled in an English village, have some touching resemblances with those of the creator of the romance. The plot of *Bianca* is tragic and the story starts with the death of Enez, Bianca's elder sister and the funeral on a cold February day. Bianca and her father mourn the death:

> They lowered the coffin. The father stood silent, his eyes half-closed, his lips trembling; was he praying? Was he weeping? Bianca's tears fell silently, drop by drop; some times a deep-drawn sigh shook her light frame; she kept down the sobs in that way.[19]

Bianca is overcome with grief and Martha, her Scottish maid, persuades her to try and forget the loss. After a year Walter Ingram, her dead sister's fiance, wants to marry her. Ingram is "a rather handsome young man of about twenty-four, with a frank countenance, fair hair and pale blue eyes," and in stature of "the middle height".[20] In the meantime, her own father has died. Ingram still loves Inez and they meet at this time Lady Moore and her son and daughter. Bianca falls in love with the son, Lord Moore. There are family objections to the marriage with Lord Moore, who goes off to the Crimean War. But before his departure, Lord Moore takes off a small ring and slids it on Bianca's marriage finger saying: "You will wear that for my sake, darling and if I ever return."[21] Here the story breaks off. A footnote by Govin Chunder at the end of the story runs as under:

> The gentle hand that had traced the story thus far... the hand of Miss Toru Dutt,...left off here. Was it illness that made the pen drop from the weary fingers? I do not know. I think not. The sketch was a first attempt probably and abandoned. I am inclined to think so because the novel left in the French language is very much superior indeed to this fragment and is complete. Other fragments there are both in prose and verse but mostly rough hewn and unpolished.[22]

Toru did not carry this fragment on because she might have felt that it was "too gloomy to continue"[23] and began her French novel.

Le Journal de Mademoiselle d' Arvers was published in 1879 by a Paris firm Didier. The French authoress, Mlle. Clarisse Bader, looked after the publication of the novel and wrote an Introduction. It was dedicated to his Excellency Lord Lytton, Viceroy and Governor-General of India, with 'temoignage de profonde recomaissance.' It is a successful and complete novel and according to one, "an extraordinary feat, without precedent".[24]

It is remarkable that in recent years two complete Bengali translations of this novel have appeared, one in 1949 by Rajkumar Mukherjee and the other in 1958 by Prithwindranath Mukhopadhyaya. The former has also published a study of Toru Dutt in Bengali, Kavi Toru Dutt (1959).

Le Journal, which consists of extracts from the dairy of a French Catholic girl, ranges over a period of a year and a half, a period beginning with her leaving the convent school, where she had been educated and ending with her premature death within the first and death is inserted as an epilogue to the diary. The novel begins with 'the pretty prattle of a young girl who has known no sorrow and whose heart is filled with pure and simple joys'. Marguerite d' Arvers is the only child of her parents...a retired General and his wife, who are now living in Brittany. She returns home in time to celebrate her fifteenth birthday. At her birthday party she meets friends whom she had known in her childhood: Madame Goserell with her two sons, Dunoins and Gaston. Three days later, a young officer, Louis Lefevre, comes on a visit to her home. He is the orphan son of old friends of Marguerite's parents. A glimpse is given of the way in which Marguerite fills up her days: in walks with her father, in tending her domestic pets and in visiting the poor and aged in the neighbouring village. She obtains a place for one of the village girls, Jeannette, as lady's maid to the Countess and later on goes herself to visit at the Chatean, where the Countess accords her a warm welcome. She there meets her hostess's brother, Colonel Desclee. Another trip which she takes is to Paris, to stay with her great-aunt Genevieve. Marguerite's parents would fain her united to Louis, but when he solicits her, she refuses him. She has fallen in love with

Count Dunois and the Countess one day discovers the fact and rejoices. Dunois and Gaston, however, are both secretly enamoured of Jeannette and in a fit of madness Dunois kills his brother. Only on recovering sanity does he become aware of his crime and also of Marguerite's love and is condemned to penal servitude. In another fit of insanity, he commits suicide and the Countess goes mad. Marguerite falls seriously ill. She feels that it is her duty to marry Louis and please her parents. Mark the following dialogue between Marguerite and her mother:

> "Do you love him now, my child?"
> "Yes, Mother."
> "More than any body else?"[25]
> "Yes, Mother."

The sisterly affection that Marguerite had at the outset for Louis develops into a deep love and the end of the story is taken up with an account of her happy days of married life at Nice, her return home and death there, leaving a little son behind. The end of Marguerite is really very pathetic:

> "Louis, are you there?" she said, unaware that it was he who was holding her. "I don't see you." He bent down towards her. "Ah! Now I can see you, my love", she said with her charming smile. Then she passed her little thin hands over her husband's face and kissed him. Her eyes were wide open; her head fell back upon the pillow. "Give me our son, Louis."
>
> He brought the child close to her face. She looked at him for a long time, then kissed him tenderly and said, "He is sleeping; I wanted to see his limpid eyes once, before we part, but never mind; put him back in his cradle, and take care that he doesn't wake up". When Louis had put the child in the cradle, she took the hand of the young father in hers and whispered, "It's quite dark. Come closer, my love. Closer", she pressed her husband's hand. "I'm tired", she murmured, "so tired...I am going to sleep now. Kiss me, my beloved, before I sleep."

He kissed her.

"God take us into his protection!" she sighed. Such, from childhood, had been her last prayer before sleeping. She closed her eyes; her lips parted slightly, and her pure soul flew thence to the bosom of God, and Marguerite slept the sleep of death.[26]

The plot of the novel is simple and elicits the reader's interest throughout. The story is told very skilfully. The novel, though originally written in French, is very different from the ordinary French novel. It has no ghastly details, no sordid or vulgar incidents, such as we often find in a French novel of the same nature. It was received with applause everywhere. James Darmesteter, Adrien Desprez, Garcin de Tassy (the eminent Orientalist) and many other French literatures and critics praised it whole-heartedly. England also joined in the chorus of praise, as is shown from the following extract:

> There is every reason to believe that in intellectual power Toru Dutt was one of the most remarkable women that ever lived. Had George Sand or George Eliot died at the age of twenty one, they would certainly not have left behind them proof of application or of originality superior to these bequeathed to us by Toru Dutt; and we discover little of merely ephemeral precocity in the attainments of this singular girl.[27]

It is indeed a book which is a marvel from the linguistic point of view. Though not an autobiography in the strict sense of the term, it reveals much of the inner life of Toru Dutt.

Toru's genius reached its culmination in *Ancient Ballads and Legends of Hindustan*, which was published in 1882 by Messrs Kegan Paul & Co., London. There are nine ballads and legends in this volume. They are: "Savitri", "Lakshman," "Jogadhya Uma", "The Royal Ascetic and the Hind," "Dhruva," "Buttoo," "Sindhu", "Prahlad" and "Sita". Apart from these, the volume also contains a few delightful poetic pieces in a separate section called "The Miscellaneous Poems". Sir Edmund Gosse wrote an "Introductory Memoir" to this collection of poems and expressed the opinion that "it will be ultimately found to constitute Toru's chief legacy to posterity".[28] A reprint of *Ancient Ballads* was brought out in 1927 by the same publisher. The first Indian reprint of the book was issued by Messrs Kitabistan, Allahabad, in 1940 with an "Introductory Memoir" by Dr. Amaranatha Jha (for more details, see the ensuing chapter).

Toru was also an excellent writer of letters. Most of her letters were directed to her Cambridge friend, Miss Mary Martin and some to the renowned French authoress Mlle. Clarisse Bader, whose love and admiration she won through correspondence. She wrote, in all, 53 letters to Mary from India. Earlier, she had, in the opinion of her biographer, Harihar Das, dropped a few letters from England and France to her relatives in India, but additional light expected to be thrown on the life and attainments of the poetess is not in our possession. The letters to Mary Martin suffice to reveal all that is feminine and childlike in Toru. They are collected in Harihar Das's monumental book, *The Life and Letters of Toru Dutt.* Clarisse Bader has spoken of Toru's letters in the following manner: "Her letters revealed a frankness, sensibility, and charming goodness and simplicity which endeared her to me, and showed the native qualities of the Hindu woman developed and transformed by the Christian civilization of Europe."[29]

In addition to these works and letters, Toru Dutt as well as her elder sister, as reported by Govin Chunder in his "Prefatory Memoir", kept diaries of their travels in Europe. It is a pity that no portion of these diaries has ever been published and it is doubtful that they can ever be traced.

Conclusion

Toru Dutt was a pioneer in the field of Indo-Anglian poetry. It is customary to begin a survey of Indo-Anglian poetry with her and indeed, she was "the first authentic Indo-Anglian".[30] Coming as she did in the wake of the cultural renaissance, the seeds of which were so assiduously sown by Derozio, Madhusudan and, above all, Rammohan Roy, Toru wrote, in the few years she was destined to live, some exquisite poetry, displaying an amazing maturity of mind and feeling.

Her poetic output is meagre, but splendid. One is only left speculating about her extraordinary talent and creative fertility which could have enabled her to reach the unexpected height of poetic achievements, had the race of her life not been so quickly run.

NOTES

1. K.R. Srinivasa Iyengar, *Indian Writing in English,* 2nd ed. (Bombay: Asia Publishing House, 1973), p. 56.
2. H.H. Anniah Gowda, "Toru Dutt and Sarojini Naidu as Poets", *The Literary Half-Yearly,* Vol. 9, No. 1 (1968), p. 19.
3. Jyotis Chandra Dass Gupta, "Toru Dutt", *National Biography for India*, 4 (1914), p. 307.
4. Margaret Macnicol, *Poems by Indian Women* (Calcutta: Y.M.C.A. Press and London: OUP., 1923), p. 37.
5. Edmund W. Gosse, "Introductory Memoir", *Ancient Ballads and Legends of Hindustan* (London: Kegan Paul & Co., 1882), p. xii.
6. *Ibid*., p. xiii.
7. Harihar Das, *The Life and Letters of Toru Dutt*, p. 112.
8. *Ibid*., p. 114.
9. *Ibid*., p. 125.
10. *Ibid*., p. 146.
11. *Ibid*., p. 159.
12. *Ibid*., p. 190.
13. *Ibid*., p. 195.
14. *Ibid*., p. 203.
15. K.R. Srinivasa Iyengar, *Indian Writing in English,* p. 63.
16. Harihar Das, *The Life and Letters of Toru Dutt,* p. 311.
17. *Ibid*., p. 304.
18. *Ibid*., p. 112.
19. Toru Dutt, *Bianca, or The Young Spanish Maiden*: Chapter 1, quoted from *The Bengal Magazine,* VI (August 1877-July 1878), p. 265.
20. *Bianca,* Chapter II; *ibid*., p. 271.
21. *Bianca,* Chapter IX; *ibid*., p. 381.
22. *Idem.*
23. Padmini Sengupta, *Toru Dutt* (New Delhi: Sahitya Akademi: 1968). p. 79.

24. Radhakamal Mukerjee, "Great Indian Women of the Nineteenth Century: Toru Dutt", *Great Women of India,* ed., Swami Madhavananda and Ramesh Chandra Majumdar (Mayavati Almora, Himalayas: Advaita Ashram, 1953), p. 402.
25. Toru Dutt, *Le Journal de Mademoiselle d' Arvers* (Paris: Didier, 1879); translated by Prithwindra Mukerjee and quote from *The Illustrated Weekly of India* (December 15, 1963), p. 43.
26. *Ibid.*, quoted from *The Illustrated Weekly of India* (December 29, 1963), p. 27.
27. *The Saturday Review*, August 28, 1879.
28. Edmund Goss, "Introductory Memoir", *Ancient Ballads and Legends of Hindustan*, p. xxii.
29. Quoted from *The Life and Letters of Toru Dutt,* p. 288.
30. K.R.S. Iyengar, *Indo-Anglian Literature,* p. 9.

A Sheaf Gleaned in French Fields

4

This was the only work which Toru saw printed and privately published during her lifetime. On its appearance, a copy was sent to the editor of the *Examiner* (London) for review. Prof. W. Minto was then the editor of this paper. Prof. Minto thrust the copy of *A Sheaf* into the unwilling hands of Sir Edmund Gosse for a review. The book belied the expectations of Sir Gosse and he reviewed it very sympathetically, though he deplored that it contained no preface or introduction.

A Sheaf was printed by the Saptahik Sambad Press at Bhowanipore in March 1876 and dedicated to Mrs. Govin Chunder Dutt (her mother). It sold out quickly. In May 1878, her father brought out its second edition with a Prefatory Memoir by him. This edition also exhausted within two years and the third one followed in 1880 published by M/s. Kegan Paul & Co., London.

Editions of the Book

The first edition was a large octavo volume of 234 pages (including 40 pages of Notes). Out of a total of 165 poems, 8 were by Aru Dutt and the remainder by Toru Dutt. These were all verse translations in English from the original French covering some seventy Parnassian poets. In all probability, the copies dispatched for foreign reviews, including those of Sir Edmund Gosse and Andre Theuriet, were paperbacks, since they were easier to pack and post. Some 44 fresh translations were added to the first edition at the time of the release of the second impression of the book, raising the total of poems to 209 in all. Govin Chunder's Prefatory Memoir to this edition is really heart-touching, especially when he gives a pen-portrait of the two sisters now in the jaws of Death. He writes thus:

> The great ambition of the sisters was to publish a novel anonymously, which Toru should write, and Aru who was far more deft at the pencil should illustrate. Toru's part of the contract has been faithfully fulfilled. I have before me her manuscript. It is in the form of a diary written in French by a young lady. The scene is laid in French, and the characters are all French men and women. I shall publish it probably hereafter. Aru did not live to complete her part of the undertaking.[1]

The novel hinted at here is *Le Journal de Mademoiselle d' Arvers*. The hard labour of Toru Dutt was ultimately rewarded when in 1880 a British publisher ventured to publish it.

Toru began translating French poems into English when she was yet in England, and continued it after her return to India. She used to publish them in the "Poet's Corner" of the *Bengal Magazine* from time to time. Her final contribution to this well-known magazine was a rendering of A Barbier's "La Cavale", which her father had discovered among her manuscripts after her premature and sad demise and which he had sent for publication therein.

Reviews of the Book

The reviews of *A Sheaf* were generally fine and favourable. The reviewers welcomed the volume in such papers and periodicals as the *Hindu Patriot,* the *Englishman,* and the *Indian Charivari.* About the notice in the *Englishman*, Toru wrote that it was "generous and candid, pointing out some mistakes in the versifying, but altogether very favourable and sincere, with some extracts from the book, namely *To Papa by Musset* and the last sonnet addressed to papa".[2] The *Indian Mirror* and the *Madras Standard* were the next to notice the existence of the book. The latter took Toru for a gentleman and the poetess was 'rather amused' and 'perhaps a little flattered' at this mistake. Many other good notice of the book appeared in the *Bengal Magazine*, *Bengalee*, and the *Friend of India.*

The foreign presses were not lagging behind in noticing the book. In August 1876, the *Examiner* of London published a two column review of it by Sir Gosse. It is partly quoted below:

> This remarkable volume seems expressly arranged to tantalize the sympathetic reviewer. It is roughly printed, and bound in paper, comes, too, from an obscure Indian Press and by no smallest preface or introduction designs to give us the least inkling of its genesis.... It is obvious, then, that to have translated pieces from the best French poets, such as might come under a pupil's notice in any ordinary school anthology, into English prose, would have been a respectable feat for an Indian girl. What, then, is our surprise, to find Miss Toru Dutt translating, in every case into the measure of the original, no less than 166 poems, some of them no less intricate in form than perplexing in matter. This amazing feat she has performed with a truly brilliant success.[3]

In one of her letters to Mary Martin, Toru comments on Sir Gosse's review of the *Sheaf*. She says, "It is rather a long notice, full two columns, and very generous and frank and a little funny too. It is the best notice that has been written on the *Sheaf*, and I thank the reviewer, whoever he may be, most heartily."[4]

E.J. Thompson also reviewed the book and observed: "Toru Dutt remains one of the most astonishing women that ever lived, a woman whose place is with Sappho and Emily Brontë, fiery and unconquerable of soul as they; and few statements, one feels, can more triumphantly sustain fair examination than this. The remarkable verses in which she chronicles the dream that foreran death go to strengthen this same conviction of power and fire.... These poems are sufficient to place Toru Dutt in the small class of women who have written English verse that can stand. The *Sheaf* is remarkable after other fashion. Merely to have translated so much and so well from one alien tongue into another must be a feat hardly paralleled; and the book contains much work that is individual and beautiful."[5] Thompson was all praise for Toru's critical acumen reflected in her scholarly notes on individual poets and poems. The French papers like *Courier de[6]Europe* and *Revue des Deux Mondes* published decent reviews of the book by Chatelain and Andre Theuriet respectively.

A Critique

A Sheaf mostly represents the Romantic school of French poets, the school which sought to express freely the thought and feeling of individuals in a moving diction and metre. In France, the main exponents of this school were Victor Hugo (the poet) and Sainte-Beuve (the critic). Others to adorn the galaxy of this school were Verlaine, Gautier, Nerval, Borel, Deschamps, Leconte de Lisle, Baudelaire, Soulary, Bouilhet, etc. Although the dominant concern of Toru in this volume is the translation of the French Romantic poets, the poets of other ages are not completely ignored. She, thus, gives us a few pieces from the poets of the transition period, such as Chenier, Courier, Beranger and Lamartine. She even goes back farther, and gives poems of Parny and de Florian of the 18th century, of Searron and P. Corneille of the 17th century and of du Bartas and du Bellay of the 16th century. Besides these, Toru translates the work of those poets who stood a little apart from the Romantic school, namely, de Vigny, de Musset, Barbiar, Brizeux, Moreau, Dupont, Mme. Ackermann and Mme. Valmore. She also includes some pieces by Heine, a Germany-born poet. Taken together, the *Sheaf* is a reliable companion to modern French poetry.

Of all the poets rendered in this volume, Victor Hugo holds the most important place with 31 pieces figuring in it. Evidently, Hugo was Toru's favourite and she allowed more space to him than to anyone else. Her renderings have succeeded in capturing the charm and delicacy of Hugo's French poems and the vigour and variety of his diction and metre. Hugo's multipronged personality peeps through them.

F. de Gramont is represented in the *Sheaf* with 17 poems and J. Soulary with 14. Their immaculate skill in sonneteering induced the translatress to give them this representation. Out of 17 pieces by Gramont selected for translation, 15 are sonnets. One of his best sonnets is "Sonnet-Freedom". Harihar

Das has also spoken of Toru's partiality for "the translation of sonnets".[7]

Among other poets, T. Gautier and Sainte-Beuve are represented by six and five pieces each, whereas Barbier, Lisle, Mme. Valmore and Lamartine by four pieces each. Other poets are represented by three or two or only one.

A cursory glance at the book convinces the reader that Toru was not doing her work with any well-planned method in mind and that is why she did not allot space to individual poets according to their established positions in French poetry. Thus, Gramont is over-represented, while Lamartine, whose place is beside Hugo, does not receive adequate attention, although the translatress thought of Lamartine and Laprade highly. Only four of Lamartine's poems and one of Laprade's are given in this volume.

Thematically speaking many of the poems in the *Sheaf* are patriotic in content, while many others deal with multiple things—doves and butterflies and swallows, homely joys and simple scenes, kindness and bravery, child life and ideal manhood.[7] The romantic side of life appealed to her imagination most. One such poem is Gensoul's "My Village", which is partly given below:

> Oh fair sky of my native land,
> How much I miss thee here!
> And thee, oh home—on sweet retreat!
> I ever held so dear.
> Canst thou not, Sun, that openest now
> The summer's treasures free,
> Give back to me my sky and home,
> My life and gaiety? (p. 40)

Hugo's "After the Battle", Gramont's "Sonnet-Freedom" and Berat's "My Normandy" are pregnant with patriotic instincts.

But Toru was more sensitive towards pathetic subjects—those that spoke of "separation and loneliness, exile and captivity, illusion and dejection, loss and bereavement, declining seasons and untimely death".[8] In many pieces we witness a lingering note of pathos and frustration. Such are the pieces of Mme. Valmore, de Musset, de Vigny, de Nerval, de Lisle, Dupont, etc.

The *Sheaf* being the work of a girl still in her teens may perhaps not interest the average reader of poetry, nor can it be expected to have attained perfection in the art of versification. But here and there we do see flashes of delicate fancy and firm hold on the subject. It may have lapses of rhyme and rhythm on and off, but it also shows the power of a true genius at work. Sir Gosse took it to be "certainly the most imperfect of Toru's writings", but he, too, conceded that "it is not the least interesting".[9]

Harihar Das thinks that Toru's command of the English language is 'wonderful' here and that "it is difficult to realize that the book is not the work of English writer".[10] Mlle, Clarisse Bader the French authoress, also remarks that Toru 'has taken her rank and place among the writers of England'. No doubt, the book has certain 'limping lines' and a few 'archaic phrases', but such defects are not too many. Very often, Toru has succeeded marvelously in capturing the metre and spirit of the original French. She, however, does not hesitate to give a twist or twang to the original if the occasion so demanded. Thus, Hugo's "Napoleon le petit" is a good specimen of her work and her substitution of 'Tom Thumb' for 'le Petit' is really ingenious and satisfying.

At times Toru completely rejected the words, phrases and sentences of the original. As an illustration, we give here after the first stanza of Beranger's "My Vocation":

> A waif on this earth,
>   Sick, ugly and small,
> Condemned from my birth
>   And rejected by all,
>   From my lips broke a cry,
>   Such as anguish may wring,

Sing,—said God in reply,
Chant poor little thing. (pp. 9-10)

Its French original reads thus:

Jete sur cette boule,
Laid, chetif, et souffrant;
Etouffe dans la foule,
Faute d'etre assez grand;
Une plainte touchante
De ma bouche sortit;
Le bon Dieu me dit; Chante,
Chante, pauvre petit! (p. 236)

In Toru's hands, the third and fourth lines suffered a sea-change and 'Une plainte touchante' of the fifth line became 'Such as anguish may wring'. However, her weakness as a translatress is also quite apparent here, especially when she substitutes 'Sing...Chant' for 'Chante' Chante. Had she given us 'Sing... Sing' in place of 'Sing...Chant', it would have been a welcome change at an appropriate place, but Toru missed at the crucial moment.

Taken as a whole, the *Sheaf* contains some really charming songs in it, such as Hugo's "Lines", Beranger's "My Vocation" and Berat's "My Normandy". Beranger's "My Vocation" was, when Toru was alive, prescribed for the Entrance Examination in Bengal. The poem "On the Death of a Young Girl" is of great interest to us, as it is deeply autobiographical boding ill of her own existence. The *Sheaf* is a literary work of which we can be proud despite its minor lapses and Harihar Das is correct in his statement when he observes that had Toru written nothing more than this, she would have left behind her something that will not soon die away.[11]

Toru's critical notes appended to the volume have been invariably praised by scholars. Sir Gosse is of the opinion that the notes "are no less curious, and to a stranger no less bewildering".[12] Her naiveté and profundity are both startling herein. Although the notes reveal her wide reading and vast learning, they suffer from certain lapses of omission and commission. She has, for instance, no idea of the death of any of her favourites and indulges in preachings where none is warranted.

Aru Dutt's Contribution to the *SHEAF*

At the end of eight pieces in the *Sheaf*, we have the initial 'A', which stands for Aru Dutt. The eight pieces by Aru are: "The Young Captive", "The Emigration of Pleasure", "Romance of Nina", "Morning Serenade", "Chanson", "My Village", "The Mother's Birthday" and "The Captive to the Swallow". This is all that Aru ever wrote though her poetic output is meager. She should have given us something more had she lived longer, she was simply twenty when she expired. She was a gifted child of Nature, no less gifted in her taste and skill than her younger sister. She was an adept at pencil (which Toru was not) and had a novel in mind to illustrate (to be written by Toru, though). The novel was *Le Journal.* Govin Chunder has thrown light on this aspect in his Prefatory Memoir.

Aru, like her sister, had an unusual lyrical talent and efficiency. She has given us "some altogether complete gems".[13] Her mind was saturated with Romanticism and her subjects are all delicate and pathetic in texture. Pathos is the hallmark of her work. She loved to indulge in the transient elements of Romantic flavour with utmost dedication.

Aru's first poem, "The Young Captive" is based on Andre Chenier's "Le Jeune Captive", the heroine of which, according to Toru, was Aimee de Coigny, Duchess de Fleury. The Duchess falls a victim to the forces of French Revolution. The whole of the poem abounds in pathetic touch and romantic imagination until the climax is struck in the penultimate stanza:

> A prisoner myself broken-hearted and crushed,
> From my heart to my lips all my sympathies rushed,
> And my lyre from its slumbers awoke;
> At these sorrows, these wishes, of a captive, I heard,

And to rhyme and to measure I married each word
As softly and simply she spoke. (p. 5)

For one eager to make comparison with the original, the French version of the above stanza is being given below:

L'epi naissant murit de la faux respecte;
Sans crainte du pressoir, le pamper tout I'ete
Boit les doux presents de I' aurora;
Et noi, comme lui belle, et jeune comme lui,
Quoi que I'heure presente ait de trouble et d'ennui,
Je ne veux pas mourir encore.

Obviously, Aru kept her renderings no less close to the original than her younger sister.

The next poem, "The Emigration of Pleasure", is also a fine piece of translation. It depicts the sorrows of France at a time when it was locked in war with European nations. A piece of five stanzas in all, it is steeped in misery and frustration.

Another poem, "Romance of Nina", is of shorted length. It became very popular when it was published. It can be sung and memorised. Its full text runs thus:

When back the well-loved shall return
    To her who pines though once so dear,
The Spring from its abundant urn
    Shall scatter blossoms far and near.
I watch, I wait;—in vain, in vain,
    The loved and lost comes not again.
Ye birds far sweeter shall ye sing
    When ye shall catch his tender tone;
Then haste the well-loved back to bring.
    I'll teach ye songs of love alone.
I watch, I wait;—in vain, in vain,
    The loved and lost comes not again.
O echo whose repose I mar
    With my regrets and mournful cries,

He comes,—I hear his voice afar,
    Or is it thine that thus replies?
Peace! hark he calls! In vain, in vain,
    The loved and lost comes not again. (p. 23)

In this poem, the beloved is quite broken and dispirited at the loss of some one really 'loved and lost'. Aru's sensitive nature lent charm and delicacy to it.

The same is true also of "Morning Serenade". It was this poem that Sir Gosse first opened and read when the *Sheaf* fell into his hands. When his initial hitch and hesitation was gone and when he read a portion of it, he was filled with 'surprise and almost rapture'. Sir Gosse was, however, wrong in attributing this poem to Toru Dutt. The critic who first discovered and revealed this fact was E.J. Thompson. It is so moving and rapturous that the entire place should be quoted here for the delight of the reader:

    Still barred the doors!—The far east glows,
    The morning wind blows fresh and free,
    Should not the hour that wakes the rose
    A waken also thee?
    No longer sleep,
    Oh, listen now!
    I wait and weep,
But where art thou?
    All look for thee, Love Light, and Song;
    Light, in the sky deep red above,
    Song, in the lark of pinion strong,
    And in my heart, true Love.
    No longer sleep,
Oh, listen now!
    I wait and weep,
    But where art thou?
    A part we miss our nature's goal,
    Why strive to cheat our destinies?

Was not my love made for thy soul?
Thy beauty for mine eyes?
No longer sleep,

Oh, listen now!
I wait and weep,
But where art thou? (p. 30)

Aru has rendered this piece in the best possible manner. Its high lyrical note and repetitive burden are deeply touching. On going through this piece, Sir Gosse rightly pronounced: "When poetry is as good as this it does not much matter whether Rouvevre prints it upon whatman paper, or whether it steals to light in blurredy type from some press in Bhowanipore".[14] Its original was Victor Hugo's "Autre Chanson".

The following three poems—"Chanson", "My Village", and "The Mother's Birthday"—are not so good as the poems already considered. Of these, "Chanson" is full of romantic longings and long-cherished dreams. "My Village" is also written in the same vein and style. The speaker is an exile, who wants to die in the land of his birth. He says:

Arise each day—My native land,
In memory's longing eye!
In thee began my course of life,
In thee I wish to die. (p. 41)

For one thing, in these poems, too, Aru's lyrical touch reaches the height of success. The third poem, "The Mother's Birthday", brings to light the celebration of Mamma's birthday out of deep love for her. The writer of this piece is not known, but it was, alone with "My Village", picked up from *Nos Souvenirs*.

The eighth and last piece by Aru is "The Captive to the Swallows", a well-known song of Beranger. It is a fine piece of rendering. A soldier is made captive and he has nobody to talk to and hence he begins speaking with the swallows from afar.

He imagines that some of them might have been born upon the roof of his own house. He asks them to give him some news about his loved native land—France. This is the last stanza to be marked for its profundity of feeling lucidity of expression:

> Who live there yet? And who have died?
>   O speak, dear birds, for you must know,—
> Who slumber happy side by side?
>   And who, as exiles, live in woe?
> My country's birds your tidings tell,
>   As high ye circle in the air,
> Though never heart for me may swell
>   Nor ever rise the mother's prayer. (p. 44)

It is clear from her contribution to the *Sheaf* that whatever Aru touched with her pen became aglow with her intense feelings and lyrical abundance. She shows a commendable command of the English language in her poems and French was she equally at home in her renderings may easily those of her sister and abound in charm and sweetness of a superior quality. It would, indeed, be amiss not to take her contribution to the *Sheaf* into account, as her poetic output is entirely contained in it.

NOTES

1. Govin Chunder Dutt, "Prefatory Memoir", *A Sheaf Gleaned in French Fields* (Bhowanipore: The Saptahik Sambad Pr., 1878), p. xi.
2. Quoted in Harihar Das's *The Life and Letters of Toru*, p. 143.
3. *The Examiner*, dated 26th August 1876.
4. Harihar Das, *op. cit.*, p. 220.
5. *Ibid.*, pp. 344-45.
6. *Ibid.*, p. 298.
7. A.N. Dwivedi, *Toru Dutt* (New Delhi: A-H, 1977), p. 137.
8. *Ibid.*, p. 38.
9. Sir E. Gosse, "Introductory Memoir", *Ancient Ballads*, p. xv.
10. H. Das, *op. cit.*, p. 301.

11. H. Das, *op. cit.*, p. 303.
12. Kalipada Mukherjee, "Aru Dutt and Her Work", *The Calcutta Review*, XL III (Apr.-June 1932), p. 198.
13. E. Gosse, "Introductory Memoir", *Ancient Ballads*, p. xvi.
14. E. Gosse, "Introductory Memoir", *Ancient Ballads*, p. x.

Toru Dutt's *Ancient Ballads and Legends of Hindustan*: A Critique

5

Toru had already predicted to bring out another *Sheaf* soon, this time gleaned in Indian fields. The prediction was made when she was absorbed in intensive course in Sanskrit. This second *Sheaf* is nothing else but *Ancient Ballads and Legends of Hindustan.* In writing this work, she was impelled by an inner urge to seek the roots for her poetic anchorage. *Ancient Ballads*, as it is, is "essentially native in genre and outlook".[1] For all her Western faith and education, Toru never ceased to be Indian. The past stories of Hindustan touched her deeply and evoked a responsive chord within her. Such ancient Indian sources as the *Ramayana, the Mahabharata, the Vishnu Purana* and *the Bhagvata Gita* gave her woman's imagination free play and she sang gaily about our old illustrious men and women. Her Christianity did not interfere with her literacy pursuits. After all, she was an Indian woman writing in a foreign medium and like Sarojini Naidu who followed her, she was perfectly 'autochthonous'. In her work there is no room for "artificiality or stimulated hot-house efflorescence".[2] Here she agreeably responded to the heart-beats of the antique racial tradition. As a child, she had heard stories of the past from her mother and nurse. Her studies in Classical Sanskrit added an edge to her interest in our ancient heritage.

Ancient Ballads was published posthumously in 1882, with an Introduction by the noted English critic Sir Edmund Gosse. Apparently, Toru had originally planned a series of nine ballads and legends for this volume, but when her father searched her papers after her death, two were missing, or possibly not written. He filled up the gap with "The Legend of Dhruva" and "The Royal Ascetic and the Hind", the two tales that she had translated from *the Vishnu Purana* and that had appeared in *The Bengal Magazine*. These two tales were, in truth, her first experiments with poetical composition in blank verse. Of the remaining ballads, it may be safely said that "Savitri", "Lakshman" and "Jogadhya Uma" are the later pieces in comparison with "Buttoo", "Sindhu", "Prahlad" and "Sita", as these last four show in no way the accomplishment of the first three.[3] They lack the fire and skill of the other ballads. However, there is a common feature in all the ballads—the employment of the octosyllabic metre. Besides trying at blank verse, Toru used pentameter in "Sindhu". On the whole, this wonderful work marked "the beginning of a new phase in the development of Toru's genius namely, her desire to give expression to her intense love of her own land and its traditions".[4]

Critics' Opinions

Ancient Ballads is a very popular work of Toru Dutt, especially "Savitri" in it. Sir Gosse welcomes it thus: "We believe that the original English poems which we present to the public for the first time today, will be ultimately found to constitute chief legacy to posterity".[5] Harihar Das thinks that it is "the best work in English" and that it "shows how Toru's intellect, while thoroughly assimilating the spirit of French and English literature, found eventually its truest expression in Sanskrit literature and this was final phase in the evaluation of the mind of this sensitive, intensely Indian poetess. This work was the result of a year's study of Sanskrit with her father after the return of the family from Europe...."[6] Another noted critic, T.O.D. Dunn, has observed thus about it: This volume, published by Messrs Kegan Paul, contains her latest best work. "It is not large in quantity, but its value is understandable. Unlike her predecessors, Toru Dutt did not willfully anglicize her ideas. For the first time in literature of this kind, there is struck a genuinely Indian note and through the medium of a perfect English expression, there is conveyed something of the sincerity of a mind proud of the intellectual traditions of its native land.... Her verse is finely knit, vigorous and of a pleasing variety. It is never obviously imitative, and moves with such freedom and independence as are inseparable from genius creative work."[7] Lotika Basu thinks that *Ancient Ballads* deserves to live as a document which 'for the first time reveals to the West the Soul of India through the medium of English poetry'.

The sound Toru Dutt scholar, B.K. Talookdar, has made the following remarks about it: "The most striking thing about the *Ancient Ballads* is that Toru is growing back into her own nation after having been alienated from it for a long while by two foreign literatures. One year's work at Sanskrit and the inspiration of her earliest recollections of stories told by her mother bring her back to the very heart of India. Here all artificiality is banned, all superficiality has disappeared, only Toru remains, with roots which have just begun growing into her own land. To ask how deep these roots would have grown is a matter of vain and melancholy speculation; it is enough to know that they are healthy and strong roots."[8] The great advocate of Indian creative writing in English, Prof. Amaranatha Jha, has spoken highly of this poetic volume. He says, "As one reads the ballads printed in this volume one is struck with the large space covered by descriptions of nature. Indeed, it may be reasonably said that had she lived longer, she would have attained distinction in narrative verse and in descriptive verse. She has a rare gift of story-telling, of arousing interest and curiosity, of creating suspense, and of drawing character. But perhaps in descriptive poetry she is even superior."[9] Radhakamal Mukerjee holds that for Toru's perfect poems, readers will have to come to *Ancient Ballads* where deficiency in scholarship was greatly overcome; and the muse, now freed from the trammels of translation, came out in a gorgeous form.[10] Dasgupta praises the novel method of presentation and the depth of thought in it. In this connection, he writes: "This novelty in presentation and thought is the result of optimistic colour. This is Indian, as well as modern, despite the fact that the poet revels in didacticism, what saves these poems from ethical prepossession is the poet's craftsmanship in the art of lyrical balladry marked with narrative simplicity."[11]

K.R. Srinivasa Iyengar is of the view that by the time Toru wrote *Ancient Ballads*, she was already "a good craftsman in verse, her feeling for words was impeccable, and eye and ear were alike trained for poetic description or dialogue. But these tales—some of them, at least were more than mere poems of action or character they trafficked with the supernatural".[12] Padmini Sengupta maintains that Toru's ballads "run much more smoothly and do not 'limp' as much as her French translations and are at the same time almost inspired".[13]

These critical opinions of various scholars convince the reader that all are one and the same in the praise of Toru's poetic power and her mastery of balladry. Unfortunately, this star of poetic horizon disappeared so soon, or she should have ranked with the great Romantics of English literature. *Ancient Ballads* immediately reveals that she belonged to the Romantic tradition of poetry. She has been called by B.N. Seal 'the first neo-romantic Bengali writer'. The dominant lyric note in her poetry may be attributed partly to her musical gift and predominantly soft feelings and partly to her intimate study of the French Romantic poets of the nineteenth century. Her literary sensibility must have been considerably influenced by this study. There is a Jane Austenean calm in her poetry. There is also a deep, nostalgic strain in it. Toru's treatment of the myths and legends of ancient India has "a romantic suggestion" and her fondness for them may be said to have introduction, "a kind of medieavalism",[14] into Indo-Anglian verse. The poetry of Toru Dutt is notable also for the feel of Indian life in an intricate tongue.

Savitri

Every poem in this volume has already captured the attention of the critical world. The first poem in it, "Savitri", narrates the troubled fortune of the princess Savitri and her courageous encounter with the God of Death. The constancy of the heroine, her chastity and her extraordinary devoting to her husband Satyavan are still considered as "the highest standard of conjugal love today".[15] It is one of the most beautiful legends in the *Mahabharata*, for it describes in an impassioned language the persistence with which Savitri pleads with Death to restore her husband's life and her pure and deep love for Satyavan is sufficient to overcome all obstacles. The story is recounted in an absorbing way and it is with breathless anxiety that the reader anticipates the final victory of Savitri. Toru is at home here in ballad form.

The ballad is in five parts. In the first part, we get information about Savitri's birth and parentage, her unusual grace, her falling in love with Satyavan and her parents' and Narad Muni's approval of her marriage with the youth of her heart. In the second, we have Savitri's marriage with Satyavan, her going to the hermitage, her constant devotion to gods and goddesses by keeping fasts vigils and by offering prayers, Satyavan's departure for the forest along with Savitri and the acute pain in Satyavan's head. In the third, the session in Death's court is shown and the decision of Yama to go himself for the soul of Satyavan is communicated. In the fourth, we are told about Yama's arrival on the death-scene, Satyavan's death proper, Savitri's persistent following of Yama and the philosophical discussions of Savitri which please Yama so much that he grants three boons, including Satyavan's life, to her. In the fifth, we learn about Satyavan's regaining of consciousness, his pleasant talk with his wife, their return to the hermitage and their happy domestic life. Let us now consider this important ballad and the events shaping it in some detail.

Savitri was the only child of the king of Madra, who lived in 'those far-off-primeval days' of Indian history when women were not 'pent in closed zenanas'. Beautiful of face and form, sunny and sweet of nature, like the maid of Browning's "Pippa Passes", Savitri was a benediction wherever she passed. To her parents she was a perfect gift with 'a nature pure as snow'. Her matchless purity and beauty are aptly described in the following lines:

> The sweet simplicity and grace,
> Abashed the boldest; but the good

God's purity there loved to trace,
Mirrored in dawning womanhood.[16]

As Savitri grew up into womanhood, her father anxiously pondered the question of her marriage, but could think of no 'fitting mate for one so pure'. He yielded at last to her persuasion of his dear wife that the matter be left with God.

Months passed and one summer morning Savitri went through the cornfields on her way to the hermitage, she saw some youths intent on sport. Among them there was one 'tall and lithe' and 'royal in port' and 'so frank noble'. She looked and looked and gave a sigh and slackened her pace. Toru's comment on this situation is remarkable:

What was the meaning—was it love?
Love at first sight, as poets sing,
Is then no fiction? (p. 40)

Savitri's choice was now made. Reaching the hermitage, she inquired about the youth and learnt that his name was Satyavan, son of Dyoumatsen, the former king of Salva, who had been deposed by his enemies and now old and blind, lived with his queen and only son as a hermit.

Savitri returned home with an unusual joy. She quickly confided her new feeling to her feeling to her mother and not long after this, Narad Muni, for whom nothing was a 'sealed book, came to the palace. Savitri's father explained to the great sage his own perplexity regarding the wisdom of his daughter's choice. To his dismay the Muni became strangely troubled and after repeated requests he declared that Satyavan was doomed to die within a year:

Upon this day as rounds the year
The young Prince Satyavan shall die. (p. 45)

Narad tried to persuade Savitri to choose another husband, which she firmly refused to do and with grave dignity declared:

Once, and once only, have I given
My heart and faith—tis past recall;
With conscience none have ever striven,
And none may strive, without a fall. (p. 47)

It Fate had allotted to her 'the miseries of a widow's life', nothing would alter the decree. She did not budge even an inch and the marriage was celebrated with great rejoicing. She came to her future home, where Savitri was graciously received by Dyoumatsen and his queen. Months of quiet happiness now followed in the fulfillment of all her homely duties, but she was troubled inwardly by the remembrance of Narad's prophecy. She now began to offer her prayers earnestly to God and to feed birds and Brahmins.

At last fateful day arrived. Savitri intensified her prayers and vigils. The day passed eventlessly. When the evening drew in, Satyavan expressed his desire to go to jungle to collect fruit and flower and return in time. Savitri, too, accompanied him. While, cutting the branches of a tree, Satyavan felt an acute headache. His axe fell down. With unique calm Savitri supported her dying husband and for hours they remained there looking 'like statues, magic-bound'.

In the meantime, there was consternation in the court of Death, for Prince Satyavan had not yet arrived. The emissaries of Death could not accomplish their mission, for Satyavan was protected by one whose radiance around prevented the approach of any 'soul of evil'. Death, therefore, decided to go personally for Satyavan's soul.

As Savitri still sat beside her dying husband, she saw a stranger slowly glide beneath the boughs, with a crown on his head and a scarlet vestment on his dark skin. She got up and enquired about his errand there. Death revealed his purpose to her, accomplished it and departed with the soul of Satyavan. Savitri softly laid down the corpse of Satyavan on the ground and quickly followed Death, heedless of Death's warning to carry out the funeral rites and sacrifices enjoined by the sacred writings. She told the God of Death that she must remain with her husband in woe or weal, whether he went somewhere on his own or whether he was carried by someone else.

Then followed the marvellous philosophical conversation between Savitri and Death. Savitri started speaking in terms of vedantic philosophy:

> I know that in this transient world,
> All is delusion,—nothing true;
> I know its shows are musts unfurled
> To please and vanish. To renew
> Its bubble joys, be magic bound
> In Maya's network frail and fair,
> Is not my aim! (p. 66)

Death or Yama, was greatly pleased with Savitri and desired her to ask for a boon but the life of Satyavan. Savitri then said:

> Well, be it so. My husband's sire,
> Hath lost his sight and fair domain,
> Give to his eyes their former fire,
> And place him on his throne again. (p. 68)

Yama granted the boon. Again Savitri entered into a conversation with Yama and tried to interpret death as love:

> Men call thee Yama—conqueror,
> Because it is against their will
> They follow thee—and they abhor
> The truth which thou wouldst aye instill.
> If they thy nature knew aright,
> O god, all other gods above?
> And that thou conquerest in the fight
> By patience, kindness, mercy, love,
> And not devastating wrath,
> They would not shrink in childlike fright

To see thy shadow on their path,
    But hail thee as sick souls the light. (p. 70)

These words buoyed up Yama, who favoured Savitri with another boon. This time Savitri demanded that her own father be blessed with a hundred sons. It was gladly granted to her. Then she applied a very persuasive logic to win Yama's heart. She begged him to allow her to live always in the midst of good persons and as there could be no better company than that of Yama, she should be permitted to be with him. Her actual words are really worth quoting:

Of all the pleasures given on earth
    The company of the good is best,
For weariness has never birth
    In such a commerce sweet and blest;
The Sun runs on its wonted course;
    The earth its plenteous treasure yields,
All for their sake, and by the force
    Their prayer united ever wields,
Oh let me, let me ever dwell
    Amidst the good, where'er it be,
Whether in lowly hermitcell
    Or in some spot beyond the sea. (pp. 71-72)

This manna-like speech of Savitri gladdened the heart of Yama and he promised to give her one more boon before he left for his own dim domain. Yama laid down no conditions this time. Savitri immediately caught the clue and demanded:

Let my Satyavan live again
    And children unto us be born,
Wise, brave, and valiant. (p. 73)

Yama loosed the knot that bound Satyavan's soul and blessed Savitri and vanished in a flame. Savitri took up her husband's soul and rushed towards the dense part of the forest where Satyavan's dead body lay motionless and stark. She reached the spot, knelt down, placed the soul upon the heart, and Satyavan woke up with a sudden start. His breathing was first slow, then it grew deeper. The pair, marching slowly, returned to the hermitage where the parents were awaiting them anxiously. Satyavan and Savitri lived long and happy. Yama's boons came true in due course of time. As for Savitri, she has become immortal among the Hindus and her name is remembered with great respect at every Hindu marriage. This is the end of the story.

to this day
Her name is named, when couples wed,
And to the bride the parents say,
Be thou like her, in heart and head. (p. 81)

Of the nine ballads in this work, "Savitri" occupies prominent place on the strength of its length and quality. On the one hand, it expounds the ideals of Indian womanhood, on the other, it highlights the essentials of vedantic philosophy. It abounds in beautiful nature-descriptions—the pompous marriage procession, the hermitage and its surroundings. Even the wild aspects of nature are not spared herein.

Harihar Das thinks that the legend of Savitri seems to augur "great future possibilities in the development of Toru Dutt's genius".[17] But he complains that the 'human thumb' is 'a crude expression in English' despite its being common in Sanskrit. He also complains that Toru uses "repetitions of a word to fill up the requisite number of syllables in a line"[18] and quotes the following as examples:

'It was that fatal, fatal speech.'
'A gleam of faint, faint hope is born.'
'Pale, pale the stars above them burned'.
'The day long, long will not appear.'

Maybe, these repetitions are outcome of an explicit purpose of the poetess to imitate Keats and his practice. Another scholar, Lotika Basu, opines that "Savitri" is the finest of the poems dealing with epic legends. She feels that Savitri in Toru's hands develops a distinct personality of her own, distinct from her husband, but this idea is quite alien to ancient Indian thought. This may be taken as one of the many divergences that Toru makes in the course of her story. There are some more obvious divergences in this book, such as those where the king expresses to the queen his desire to find a perfect partner for Savitri, where Narad Muni comes to the king's palace and where Savitri first meets Satyavan.

Lakshman

The next story in *Ancient Ballads* is "Lakshman", which is cast in the form of conversation between Sita and Lakshman. Rama had enraged the sister of Ravana by refusing to reciprocate her love pranks towards him. To avenge her wrong, Ravana, the chief of demons, persuaded Maricha to assume the shape of a golden deer and come roaming about the hermitage where Rama, Sita, and Lakshman lived in the forest. Deeply moved by the golden beauty of this deer, Sita begged Rama to get it for her and despite Lakshman's warnings Rama went off in pursuit, leaving his wife in his brother's charge, with strict instructions not to leave her at any cost. Rama could shoot at the elusive deer after a long pursuit and the deer made a terrible sound, sprang into the air before it came to the ground in its natural form. Maricha, however, had done all possible as per Ravana's injunctions to him. He began to roar with piercing cries: "Oh, Sita', 'oh, Lakshman'. Sita heard the cry and urged Lakshman to rush up to the rescue of his brother. It is at this point that the story actually starts. In her fear, Sita speculates that Rama is terribly hurt by his enemies and that he is now struggling for life. She scolds Lakshman for his lethargy and inaction at this moment:

> Swift in decision, prompt in deed,
>   Brave upto rashness, can this be
> The man to whom all looked at need
>   Is it my brother that I see? (p. 82)

But Lakshman speaks highly of Rama's valour and asks her to give up her ill-founded fears. He tells her that demons, ghosts and gods are equally afraid of his might and that the cry may be a trick of the foe. But Sita blames him on different grounds, including cowardice. She attributes his reluctance to go to a baser motive, accusing him of desiring Rama's death so that he may take possession of his wife and kingdom. She humiliates him with the final declaration:

> Learn this—whatever comes may come,
> But I shall not survive my love—
> Of all my thoughts here is the sum!
> Witness it gods in heaven above. (p. 86)

Lakshman is unable any longer to bear her taunts and bids her hear him once before he goes. She has cruelly wronged him by her accusations and thrown all norms of decorum to the winds. In going away from her, he disregards the plainest orders of his chief—Rama—but he himself will bear all the responsibility for his crime. Before he goes, he draws a magic circle on the ground with his arrow, asking her not to go beyond it lest she should come to harm. He acquits her of all blame and invokes a blessing on her before he departs, confident of a speedy return both of himself and of his brother. His departure is attended by ill-omens.

The poem "Lakshamn" is not properly but a dramatic dialogue. There are prosodic lapses in it, as when Sita spoils the effect of fine opening lines by

> Oh hasten, to his succour fly,
> No more hast thou, dear friend, a choice. (p. 82)

Harihar Das observes that the poem marks a departure from its predecessors in that "it is not narrative, but conversation" and finds its tone "dignified, rising sometimes to the heroic".[19] This is decidedly a correct estimate of the poem. For one thing, the poem opens casually and ends casually. For a full knowledge of the story, the reader will have to go to the original *Ramayana*.

The poem presents an insight into the strength of the bonds that bind the members of an Indian family. Harihar Das remarks that "Nowhere, we think, outside Indian thought, could we get so perfect a picture of brotherly loyalty"[20] and he is perfectly right. Lakshman remains loyal to the instructions of Rama and is not ruffled by the accusations of Sita. We know that Sita is not the Sita of the *Ramayana*, a perfect epitome of virtue, but a woman of the common rank.

The gradual working out of Sita's passion forms the most interesting feature of the poem. The opening verses convey to us a vivid impression of Sita's anxiety on Rama's behalf and her excited appeals Lakshman. The latter's fine justification of his elder brother's indomitable courage and his absolute faith in his power, serve merely to set Sita at bay. The implied reproach for her lack of faith, containing a germ of truth, causes her to turn fierce upon who meant only to comfort. She badly accuses him and applies the truly feminine weapon of bitter sarcasm. This ballad, no doubt, contains a skilful attempt at psychological delineation of character, simple and experimental, but still showing a phase of Toru's genius with which we might otherwise have been unacquainted.

Jogadhya Uma

The ensuing ballad, "Jogadhya Uma", is marvellous in its dreamy and mystic beauty. Its subject is drawn upon folklore,[21] not on any old legend. It was told to Toru by her old family nurse, Suchee, of whom all the children were very fond. This poem begins with the description of a pedlar walking along the road to Khirogram in the early morning. He was then crying thus:

> Shell-bracelets ho! Shell-bracelets ho!
> Fair maids and matrons come and buy! (p. 90)

In the early hours of the morning, there were few to hear his cry. Then, a bend in the road brought him to a lonely place where lay a beautiful tank shadowed by fruit trees. On the one side of this tank, a wide flight of marble steps ran entrance arch down to the water's edge where facing the morning light sat a lovely maiden with arresting eyes and long, dark hair. The pedlar stopped to show her his wares. His bracelets, he told her, were charms to 'keep a lover true and widowhood avert'. As the maiden looked at them and stretched her creamy hand, the pedlar slipped a bracelet on the slender wrist, marvelling at her extraordinary beauty. As he watched her hold the bracelet up against the light, an indefinable air of royal dignity about her filled him with awe. She tossed about her hair which filled him with wonder. She tossed aside the stray curls from her face and brow, as she asked the price of the bracelet, then bade him seek payment at her home. He enquired where that was. She told that her father, who would pay the bracelet, was an old priest and lived in the temple whose lofty gilded spire appeared in the distance. If he (the father) said that he had no money, the pedlar was to ask him to open the vermilion-streaked box near the shrine, where the money would be found. With his wares the pedlar went to her bidding and the maiden prepared to plunge into 'the waters pure'.

Following the directions given to him, the pedlar easily reached the temple, where cattle, flowers and tinkling bells spoke in a language sweet and plain. Suddenly he cried out, 'Shell bracelets ho' and in response a hospitable old priest came out and invited him to share in the temple feast. The pedlar gratefully accepted the proffered hospitality and then explained the errand on which he had come. Hearing the errand, the priest retorted:

> No daughter in the world have I,
> An only son is all my stay;
> Some minx has played a trick, no doubt,
> But cheer up, let thy heart be gay,
> Be sure that I shall find her out. (p. 96)

But the pedlar reassured the priest that the maiden, with such a divine face, was incapable of deceit. As a future proof of his story, he repeated the directions concerning the vermilion-streaked box. The priest wonderingly fetched the box, opened it and beheld in it the exact sum needed to pay for the bracelet. In a flash, he realised that the goddess whom he had so long sought for had come suddenly to the simple pedlar.

The pedlar also realised it and remembering the awe-inspiring beauty of the maiden, he hastily dropped the basket and set out at full speed for the tank, followed by the priest. But they met disappointment there, for nothing but a solitary heron stood sentinel in the hush which seemed to have fallen over the face of Nature. As the pedlar and the priest turned sadly away, the chime of the temple bells pealed out and they pleaded with the goddess for some sign of her presence. As they waited anxiously, there was a sudden stir in the water and a beautiful rounded arm wearing the white bracelet appeared above for an instant. Quickly the arm sank down in the water. The priest and the pedlar bowed to 'the mystic power' and before they turned back homeward they picked a lotus bird to be treasured 'in memory of the day and spot'. Ever since that day, the descendants of the pedlar have annually paid shell-bracelets of the old design as a tribute to the temple. In this way, they still acknowledge the gratitude they felt towards the goddess who had, from that eventful day, crowned their industry with success.

In writing the ballad, Toru shows the best kind of creative originality that can be thought of. How aptly she has turned a folk-story into a delightful poem. There is, indeed, an antique flavour about it. One cannot fail to mark the translucent simplicity of touch in it. It is difficult to accept the verdict of Lotika Basu when she remarks: "The Indian atmosphere of the poem is sometimes spilt by the rather jarring introduction of Priest's house which is anything but a scene that seems to be more English than Indian."[22] It is not proper to call it 'English' only on the basis of a word like 'manse'. It is likely that Toru had not yet fully forgotten her English associations. But the content, setting and the treatment are all essentially 'Indian'. Toru has suggested even the possible source of this story:

Absurd may be the tale I tell,
    Ill-suited to the marching times,
I loved the lips from which it fell,
    So let it stand among my rhymes. (p. 100)

This source is absolutely the Indian source. Harihar Das correctly considers it as "a gem of art among the *Ballads of Hindustan*".[23]

The Royal Ascetic and the Hind

The next ballad, "The Royal Ascetic and the Hind", narrates the failure of the life of asceticism. It centres round the matchless asceticism of King Bharat of Saligram. Bharat left behind all his royal luxuries at home and went out to a forest to lead an austere life there. He practised religious penances and rude privations and offered constant prayers and oblations in order to attain a perfect control on his soul. Suddenly, a change came over his mind. He once went to the river for his bath, after which he sat down on the bank for musings and prayer. Meanwhile, a beautiful pregnant hind came there to take water. She heard a lion's roar then and leapt to death and her offspring tumbled from her womb into the flowing water and struggled for life there. The king was deeply touched by the scene before him. He got up at once, drew the new born creature from the wave, and brought it home. Thenceforth he developed deep love for it and cared little even for his devotions. After many years, when Death visited him, Bharat's heart was still filled with anguish at leaving his little fawn and not with the problem of Death and Eternity:

To it devoted was his last, last thought,
Reckless of present and of future both. (p. 105)

The poem ends with a spirited defence of the hermit-king's conduct and a condemnation of the ideal of asceticism. In it Toru reads a little lecture to the ascetics for their renunciation of the world. Here she is "altogether modern, and out of the line with the past".[24] She goes so far that she forgets altogether that she is dealing with an old legend—her main purpose. In doing so she is both native and interesting. She has been able to assert her individuality and modern outlook life. The sermon that she wants to impart to the reader may well be found in the last lines:

> Not in seclusion, not apart from all,
> Not in a place elected for its peace,
> But in the heat and bustle of the world.
> 'Mid sorrow, sickness, suffering and sin,
> Must he still labour with a living soul,
> Who strives to enter through the narrow gate. (p. 106)

Rich in moral tone, they are not without a fine poetic appeal. The ballad retains the dialogue form of the original—the *Vishnu Purana*, but it serves very little purpose.

The Legend of Dhruva

Like the previous legend, "The Legend of Dhruva" is also taken from the *Vishnu Purana* (Book I, Chapter XI). It relates the story of a prince, the son of a less favoured queen (Suneetee), who spurned the position of worldly power for the sake of spiritual greatness. That prince was Dhruva, an ambitious, indignant child who was anxious to win his father's love. Suruchee, the favoured queen, did not like this because she wanted that the King's love be solely reserved for their own son, Uttama. One day, she saw Dhruva in the King's lap and angrily asked him to give up his proud ambition. At this Dhruva trembling with rage and indignation ran to his mother's room where:

> With a swelling heart
> Repeated to his mother every word
> That proud Suruchee spake, from first to last,
> Even in the very presence of the king. (p. 109)

The helpless Suneetee heard all and sighed deeply and tried to console her son, explaining to him the Hindu doctrine of *Karma*:

> The deeds that thou hast done,
> The evil, haply, in some former life,
> Long, long ago, who may alas! Annul,
> Or who the good works not done, supplement
> The sins of previous lives must bear their fruit.
> The ivory throne, the umbrella of gold,
> The best steed, and the royal elephant
> Rich caparisoned must be his by right
> Who has deserved them by his virtuous acts
> In times long past. Oh think at this my son,
> And be content. (pp. 109-10)

She also held out to him the prospect of future rewards in case he lived his present life well, and advised him:

> Be meek, devout, and friendly, full of love,
> Intent to do good to the human race
> And to all creatures sentient made of God; (p. 111)

Dhruva found little consolation in his mother's words. Far from choosing humility as his goal, he declared to her his unalterable resolve:

> I shall try
> The highest good, the loftiest place to win,
> Which the whole world deems priceless and desires. (p. 111)

So saying, he left his father's house, never to return and went to the woods to live among the hermits and fulfilled his resolve by finding 'the highest heavens', where he still 'shines a star' and where men see him in their nightly walks.

"The Legend of Dhruva" is based on the Hindu theory of *Karma*. The treatment of the legend of Dhruva has failed to create in the reader the right impression of the young boy, who, being rudely shocked at his royal father's cruel neglect of him, retired to the forest and later became a great devotee of God. The poem fails even to suggest the conflict in the aggrieved mind.[25] Harihar Das remarks that the impression left on our minds should be one of admiration for a boy, who, wise beyond his years, saw that the only thing that really counted was not place or power, but holiness of life. Instead, we are left in a state of moral perplexity, because the child's determination to avenge the slight from which he suffered by gaining a higher position in the world's esteem than the one held by his father or by his brother is to be carried out 'by prayer and penance'. The poem is a failure in artistic terms because the poetess has failed to be in line with either the present or the past. And also, it exhibits no originality on the part of the poetess. *Buttoo* the ballad that follows—"Buttoo" (or "Ekalavya") is derived from one of the stories in the *Mahabharata.* For its hero, it has a low-born hunter's son. One day, Dronacharya, the matchless master of magic and archery, sat in the forest surrounded by his pupils, a youngman with 'kindling eyes' came there and urged him to teach him the tricks of archery as to the others. On being questioned, he disclosed his name, caste and parentage. He told the master that he knew no fear in the world. At this the great master let loose a magic arrow that felled Buttoo to the ground amid derisive laughter of the princess present there. Red with shame, he left them, but was determined to show that worth was something independent of caste or creed or rank. He retired to a beautiful retreat in the thickest part of the jungle and began to learn Nature's secrets. He built a house of mud and reeds and leaves there, stores it with forest corn, fruit and nuts. He then made a perfect statue of earth representing Dronacharya and placed a bow and steel-tipped arrows, wreathed with flowers, at its feet. His exemplary courage and steadfastness ultimately bore fruits for him and he soon learnt all the secrets of magic and archery. One evening, as he practised his archery, his bow proved false and his arrow went astray twice. At the same time, he heard the barking of a wild dog, which augured an evil omen. His weapons failed him again and again. At last, he let fly a magic shaft which silenced the sound, but brought about his undoing. On that very day, Dronacharya's pupils, the Pandava and Kuru princes, were hunting in the woods and the brave Arjuna chanced upon the wild dog. In utter desperation, he sought out Dronacharya, who had promised that no other pupil besides himself should learn the secret of magic shafts and accused him of betrayal of faith. But the master reassured Arjuna and accompanied him to the hut of Buttoo, who, on being asked, revealed all about his hard practice and unique skill in archery. He told that he was a pupil of Dronacharya and looked to him as the source of all his inspiration. On hearing this, Dronacharya enquired if he were willing to yield him, as master, a pupil's due obedience. Thereupon Buttoo eagerly avowed:

> All that I have, O Master mine,
> All I shall conquer by my skill,
> Gladly shall I to thee resign
> Let me but know thy gracious will. (p. 123)

He was taken at his word, though with evident reluctance on Dronacharya's part. The master, having given promise to Arjuna, demanded his due: 'Give me, O youth, thy right-hand thumb'. Buttoo's loyalty did not waver even at this and in a moment the sharp knife severed the thumb, undoing his life-work. The master was profoundly touched by the matchless loyalty of the pupil and before he left he blessed Buttoo as under:

> Fame
> Shall sound thy praise from sea to sea,
> And man shall ever link thy name
> With self-help, Truth, and Modesty. (p. 104)

This is the summary of the story.

"Buttoo" is quite neat and clean in structure. There are few weak lines in it and when these lines are found in it, they are guilty of mannerism and not of jingle, as in the following:

> And lo—a single, single tear. (p. 114)

It has been suggested that the comparatively long and untruthful descriptions of the forest scenes through which Buttoo passes are rather not needed. But perhaps the purpose of such descriptions is to acquaint the reader with the fact that a man living in close proximity of Nature draws his strength and inspiration direct from her. And technically, the poem is "one of the happiest and least affected"[26] of Toru's compositions. In the view of Harihar Das, "under the circumstances, the reader is a little jarred by the unexpectedness of the description of Buttoo's attitude at the crucial moment of this test for obedience...."[27]

But this attitude is not unexpected since it is only normal human behaviour to react thus to a demand which revealed nothing but a spirit of mean vengeance. The teacher in Dronacharya failed the moment he demanded Buttoo's thumb. The pupil was now disillusioned, for he now realised that the man of his worship was really incapable of rising above petty considerations. For him it was a shock too deep for tears. It is, however, doubtless that politics was held above morality in those days. Buttoo gave a superb example of patience and faithfulness by leaving the entire matter to his God, who alone was competent to judge the right from the wrong.

Sindhu

"Sindhu" is the story of an ideal son in three parts. Sindhu was the only child of his sage-parents, who lived in the forest shades. The parents were blind, weak and helpless and Sindhu was their sole prop. He devoted his whole life to ministering to their needs regularly. All the peevishness and querulousness of old age was met by patience and sweetness on his part for he loved to be 'their slave'.

In part II, King Dasarath's hunting in the forest is described. One day, Dasarath organised a hunt in the forest, which rang with the blare of the trumpets. The king had lost his way and stood at a bend of the river, watching the sunset hues fade away upon the water and the gleam of silver scales, as fish leapt up in the twilight. As the darkness fell, he heard the sound as of a roebuck drinking. Immediately he shot an arrow and was startled to hear 'a feeble human wail' and in alarm rushed in the direction of the sound. There, with his pitcher at his side, he found Sindhu dying. The king, filled with remorse, tried his best to resuscitate Sindhu, but in vain. He was afraid of a 'Brahmin's dying curse'. Opening his eyes, Sindhu read the king's fear on his face and comforted him with the assurance that he knew the deed was done unwittingly. Sindhu told him that he accepted his fate as a proper punishment for a sin once committed, when he had killed one of a pair of doves that rested in a peepal tree. He revealed to him: 'Blood calls for red blood still'. For his own part, he was not loth to die, but was deeply troubled for his helpless parents. As a last favour, he urged the king to carry the pitcher down the steep lane to the hut among the trees. He 'pointed—ceased—then sudden died'. The king took up the corpse and the pitcher and moved towards the hut.

Part III shows that the parents had become anxious at Sindhu's long absence. A premonition of evil overcame the mother just as the king drew near, bearing Sindhu's dead body. At the rustling of the leaves underfoot, the old Muni joyfully exclaimed:

> Lo, here he is—oh wherefore grieves
> Thy soul, my partner dear? (p. 139)

Hearing the words, the king stopped dead in deep distress, while questions rained on him from the old pair. His stifled sob reached their ears and with it came the conviction that this was not Sindhu. The king narrated all the tale to the parents and laid the dead boy in their arms. The old pair, heart-broken and dispirited, bade him guide them to their bed of moss, for life had now no meaning for them. The king guided them where they had desired and watched beside them until the feeble flame of life flickered out. But before the old Muni died, he had predicted that Dasarath, too, should one day die 'for a son's unkindly loss'. Thereafter all the three dead bodies were brought to the river Sarayu, where the funeral rites were performed with royal pomp. In due course of time, the old Muni's prediction came true. Those who want to know more about the story, the poetess points out, should go and read the *Ramayana*. Mr. Kotoky says that the omission of the last stanza of the poem would have created "a better poetic effect and a deeper sense of completeness".[28] It is possible that the last stanza was written not so much for the well-equipped Indian readers as for the half-informed Westerners and as such it serve as a good guide for them.

"Sindhu" deals with the eternal theme of parental love. Here again the *Karma* theory has been propounded—Sindhu had killed a dove and hence his punishment. Neither he nor his parents (bearing the prediction) curse Dasarath. The poem is in ballad metre and Toru has tried to keep her language as simple as possible. The poem succeeds "only in patches".[29] There are crude inversions for the sake of rhyme in it. It is unfortunate that goggerel intrudes at those crises in the poem where it is most intolerable. As Sindhu is struck down, we read:

> Ah me: What means this?—Hark, a cry,
>   A feeble human wail,
> "Oh God:" it said—"I die, I die,
>   Who'll carry home the pail?" (p. 131)

It is true that simplicity is a characteristic of good poetry, as in the classic instance of Wordsworth's "Lucy Poems", but such passages as this one turn pathos into bathos. Toru Dutt, however, displays her genuine poetic in the description of the hunt in the forest. The description of the closing in of darkness upon the river scene is also good, though marred by an inconsistency, for darkness is said to settle 'like a pall/The eye would pieces in vain'.

Judging from the style, which is distinctly inferior to that of the other poems, we should place it as an early attempt with "The Legend of Dhruva" and "The Royal Ascetic and the Hind". There is hardly a defence to the fact that the standard of poetry in it sinks to a low level.

Prahlad

"Prahlad", taken from the *Mahabharata*, is the story of king Heerunkasyapu, who had been 'a terror both of gods and men', his audacity reached the farthest limit when he tore the *Vedas* into shreds, forbade sacrifices to the gods, slew holy men and ordered that all men should worship him and alone. The small remnant of Brahmins and pundits fled to the woods and caves and therein secret carried on the worship of the gods, who they hoped, would in due time assuage their wrongs. The tyrant's one weakness was his love for four children—Rahd, Onoorahd, Prahlad, and Sungrahd. He took some trouble to secure for them a suitable tutor. This tutor, Sonda Marco by name, was famed for his worldly wisdom for he knew how to 'trim his sail' and 'veer his bark to any winds that blew'. The children were sent to him to be taught all they needed to know, but Sonda Marco was sternly forbidden to teach them anything of the soul or of the gods. All were quick to master the lessons, but Prahlad was the most thoughtful among them. One day, the tutor heard Prahlad discussing forbidden themes among the boys and ordered him not to think of such things, but the pupil remained firm in his faith. Not long after this, the four boys were summoned to the court for a test. All went well till Prahlad's turn came. He was asked to explain 'the cream of knowledge'. The boy's reply was:

That is true knowledge which can show
The glory of the living gods—
Divest of pride, make men below
Humble and happy, though but clods.

That is true knowledge which can make
Us mortals saintlike holy, pure,
The strange thirst of the spirit slake
And strengthen suffering to endure.

That is true knowledge which can change
Our very natures with its glow,

The sciences what'er their range
Feed but the flesh, and make a show. (p. 149)

In great anger, Kasyapu commanded Prahlad:

Bow down thou slave,
And worship me, or though shalt die; (p. 150)

Prahlad, however, remained unshaken in his conviction and boldly proclaimed his views:

The gods who made us are the life
Of living creatures, small and great;
We see them not, but space is rife
With their right presence and their state.

They are the parents of us all,
'Tis they create, sustain, redeem,
Heaven, earth and hell, they hold in thrall,
And shall we these h'gh gods blaspheme? (p. 151)

Hearing this, the king, in great anger, called forth the Captain of the lifeguards and instructed him to take the adamant boy to a dungeon-cell, where he was to await the executioner. Before long, the report came to the king that the sword had refused to do its work. The court was summoned in great hurry and the failure of the sword was attributed to some magic power exercised by Prahlad. It was decided that the boy be thrown down a precipice or buried alive in sand. But these and several other devices failed to compass the prince's death. Once again Prahlad was called to the court. The proud father flung a challenge to the gods, hearing which Prahlad revealed a newly learnt truth:

There is one God—one only,—mark!
To him is all our service due. (p. 155)

and future:

> I fear not fire, I fear not sword,
> All dangers, father, I can dare;
> Along, I can confront a horde,
> For oh! My God is every where! (p. 156)

The king mockingly enquired whether God was in the crystal pillar against which he leaned. Prahlad replied in affirmative. Thereupon the king gave a hard blow to the pillar, which came tumbling down. Out of it sprang a stately sable warrior of immense stature. He had a lion's head and eyes and a human body, feet and hands. With a horrible roar, he struck the tyrant on the helm and ripped him down and hailed Prahlad as king of all the realm and then vanished in a thunder clap. At that time:

> One king lay stiff, and stark, and dead.
> Another on the peacock throne
> Bowed reverently his youthful head. (p. 157)

The trumpets rang aloud to mark great rejoicings.

In "Prahlad", the story is successfully told. The technique of the poem is "far in advance of that of the earlier poems".[30] Very rarely do we meet the false rhyme (as in 'heart' and 'thwart') or a line which mars the poetic effect by its colloquialism (e.g. 'Or there will come a fearful crash'). The poem reveals, too, a growing skill in selection on the poetess's part. The phraseology employed by Prahlad in his defence sometimes smacks of a Biblical flavour. His speeches are, by all means, individualistic and interesting throughout.

The poem would have finished more fittingly at the point where it picture, Prahlad the new-crowned king, bowing his head reverently on throne amidst the applause of the people and leaving out the apostrophe to tyrants in general. The apostrophe decidedly shows Toru's propensity for didacticism.

Sita

"Sita" is the final ballad in the volume; it is very short in length as compared with other ballads. It describes a scene frequent in Toru's childhood when she and her brother and sister used to gather near their mother in the twilight and listen to the old, sad story of Sita's unmerited sufferings at the hands of Rama. In the forest, where Sita is supposed to be after her exile, there is a clearing which is hardly ever visited by the sunlight and which is completely covered up with gigantic creepers, flowers and trees. White swans are seen gliding on a quiet lake. While the peacock rises 'whirring from the brake' and the wild deer bounds across the glades. The gold of the forest corn glints in the distance, where the blue smoke rises from the altars near the dwelling of Valmiki, the 'poet anchorite'. This is the background of the poem.

In terms of art "Sita" is among the best of all that Toru has ever written. It is simple and vivid in style and is deeply touched with a delicate pathose especially in the last lines:

> Then shall those children by their mother's side,
> Gather, ah me as erst at eventide? (p. 159)

The poem also brings to light the poetess's keen sense of observation of natural beauty (as one may find around the hut of the 'poet anchorite').

Ancient Ballads, as a whole, contains narratives loaded with lyrical profusion of joy and sorrow, anger and pathos, hope and frustration. But such a profusion does not, in any way, retard the flow of the stories of the past. From the volume it looks that the pathetic scenes and events appealed to the poetess most. Possibly it had something to do with what she saw at her home and what she herself suffered patiently. Her tragic case reminds one of the great Romantic poet, Keats.

For one thing, Toru is thoroughly Indian in this book. There are some beautiful scenes and sights of the native land in it. The ballads are steeped in Hindu ideals and sentiments and give a vivid picture of Indian life and customs. They are fundamentally about Toru's own race and country. No conscious attempt has been made at expressing thought or tradition alien to her people and culture. The sententious remarks interspersed in the ballads suggest Toru's familiarity with the best expositions of the Hindu view of life. This is what she makes Savitri say:

I know that in this transient world
All is delusion,—nothing true;
I know its shows are mists unfurled
To please and vanish. To renew
Its bubble joys, be magic bound
In Maya's network frail and fair,
Is not my aim! (p. 66)

and again:

I know in such a world as this
No one can gain his heart's desire,
Or pass the years in perfect bliss;
Like gold we must be tried by fire;
And each shall suffer as he acts
And thinks,—his own sad burden bear. (p. 67)

Of all the poems contained in the volume "Savitri" is the nearest to the Indian temper and the most articulate expression of Vedantic philosophy. The fatalistic doctrine of the popular Hindu philosophy is expressed in the following:

It is my destiny,
O fear not thou, but pity one
Whose fate is thus to die. ("Sindhu", p. 133)

The doctrine of *Karma* finds an outlet in the following passage:

The deeds that thou hast done,
The evil, haply, in some former life,
Long, long ago, who may alas annul,

Or who the good works not done, supplement;
The sins of previous lives must bear their fruit.

The ivory throne, the umbrella of gold,
The best steed, and the royal elephant
Rich caparisoned, must be his by right
Who has deserved them by his virtuous acts
In times long past. Oh think on this, my son,
And be content. (pp. 109-10)

It is from Dhruva's mother consoling the boy. E.J. Thompson is far from truth when he observes that there are only "scattered beauties" in the ballads and that Toru "stands outside her themes and does not enter deeply into them".[31] He further observes: "Nor can I consider those themes as of anything like first-class value. Some have a rustic charm which strikes the mind pleasantly enough, but not deeply; others had been handled ages before Toru took them up, by writers whose minds primitive, as hers emphatically was not, and in sympathy, as hers again was not".[32] These observations are not quite just. Toru has not only 'entered deeply' into her themes, but also handled the delicate stories efficiently in a foreign tongue. Her prosody might have occasionally faltered, but her themes do not. If the ballads sometimes read like translation, as Sir Edmund Gosse complained, that is owing to the poet's concern to be true to their original in Sanskrit. Largely objective in the treatment of her themes, Toru has yet imparted to them an imaginative touch, as in case of "Jogadhya Uma". Moreover, the stories have been told with utter sympathy and in consonance with ancient Hindu ideals.

There are some beautiful sketches of Indian life and scenery in *Ancient Ballads* which are as faithful as poetic. Here are the people stirring out early in the day in an Indian village:

A ragged herd-boy, here and there,
    With his long stick and naked feet:
A ploughman wending to his care,
    The field from which he hopes the wheat:

An early traveller, hurrying fast
    To the next town; an urchin slow
Bound for the school; these heard and past.
    Unheeding all,—"Shell-bracelets ho!"
("Jogadhya Uma", p. 91)

And here is the charming night in an Indian forest:

Under the faint beams of the stars
    How beautiful appeared the flowers,
Light scarlet, flecked with golden bars
    Of the palasas, in the bowers
That nature there herself had made
    Without the aid of man. At times
Trees on their path cast densest shade,
    And nightingales sang mystic rhymes
Their fears and sorrows to assuage. ("Savitri", p. 80)

There are several graphic descriptions of Nature in the volume. The following passage may be marked in this regard:

What glorious trees: The somber saul
On which the eye delights to rest,
The batel-nut,—a pillar tall,
With feathery branches for a crest,
The light-leaved tamarind spreading wide,
The pale faint-scented bitter neem,
The seemul, gorgeous as a bride,
With flowers that have the ruby's gleam,

The Indian fig's pavilion tent
In which whole armies might repose,
With here and there a little rent,
The sunset's beauty to disclose,
The bamboo bought that sway and swing
'Neath bulbuls as the south wind blows

The mango-tope, a close dark ting,
Home of the rooks and clamorous crows,

The champak, bok, and South-Sea pine,
The nagessur with pendant flowers
Like ear-rings,—and the forest vine
That clinging over all, empowers,
The sirish famed Sanskrit song
Which reveal maidens love to wear,
The peepul giant-like and strong,
The bramble with its matted hair,
All these, and thousands, thousands more,
With helmet red, or golden crown,
Or green tiara, rose before
The youth in evening's shadows brown.
He passed into the forest,—there
New sights of wonder met his view,
A waving pampas green and fair
All glistening with the evening dew.

("Buttoo", pp. 115-16)

What we have quoted here is only a portion of a long and vivid description of Nature. In fact, the *Champak* and the lotus and the *Kokil* always stirred the inmost of Toru's heart and she burst into delightful songs. She was keenly sensitive to sound and sight, to natural charms and to catching colours. In all this she was like Wordsworth, Keats and Shelley. Temperamentally, she was closer to these poets than to anyone else.

As one reads the ballads, one comes across some charming sketches of Indian social life and reflections on certain social problems. Mark the following passage in this connection:

And think upon the dreadful curse
    Of widowhood; the vigils, fasts,
And penances; no life is worse
    Than hopeless life,—the while it lasts,

Day follows day in one long round,
    Monotonous and bland and drear;
Less painful were it to be bound
    On some bleak rock, for aye to hear—
Without one chance of getting free—
    The ocean's melancholy voice! ("Savitri", p. 46)

The modern women's 'lib' movement gets an impetus when the following lines are read with a proper understanding:

In those far-off primeval days
    Fair Indian's daughters were not pent
In closed zenanas. ("Savitri", p. 33)

That women enjoyed full freedom of movement in ancient India is marvellously mentioned here. Sir Gosse pays only a well-merited tribute to Toru Dutt when he remarks: "No modern oriental has given so strange an insight into the conscience of the Asiatic as is presented in the stories of 'Prahlad' and of 'Savitri', or so quaint a piece of religious fancy as the ballad of 'Jogadha Uma".[33]

The modern turn given to some of these ancient legends is a feature not least attractive in itself and it contributes to their strong appeal to the readers of this day. The story of "Prahlad" suggests a political moral which might have served as a motto for a Parisian mob in the French Revolution:

The echoes rang from hill to hill,
"Kings rule for us and in our name".
Tyrants of every age and clime
Remember this,—that awful shape
Shall startle you when comes the time,
And send its voice from cape to cape.
As human peoples suffer pain,
But oh, the lion strength is theirs,
Woe to the king when galls the chain;
Woe, woe, their fury when he dares. (p. 157)

The same strong feeling of Democracy bursts out, with the passionate spirit of a Burns, in the lines:

> No matter,—what is rank or caste?
> In us honour, or disgrace,
> Not out of us.... ("Buttoo", p. 114)

Here is the true picture of a self-seeking politician:

> A man
> Among the flatterers in the court
> Was found, well-suited to the plan
> The tyrant had devised. Report
> Gave him a wisdom owned by few,
> And certainly to trim his sail,
> And veer his bark, none better knew,
> Before a changing adverse gale. ("Prahlad", p. 145)

This is the description of Sonda Marco.

Ancient Ballads presents "certain subtle character portrayals"[34] through dramatic speeches in it. Savitri, Sita and Jogadha Uma are the ideal representatives of Indian womanhood and give us an opportunity to peep into the mysterious feminine nature. In fact, Toru excels in portraying women characters. Amongst the male characters in this book are Satyavan, Lakshman, Bharat, Dhruva, Buttoo, Sindhu and Prahlad.

The book abounds in simplicity of verse and clarity of expression. The following lines from "Savitri" give us an idea of the style of Toru's writing:

> What was the meaning—was it love?
> Love at first sight, as poets sing,
> Is then no fiction? (p. 40)

Toru's sensitiveness and the worship of the Beautiful come close to the poetic spirit of Keats, the author of *Endymion.* When Savitri utters:

In the meek grace of virgin hood
    Unblanched her cheek, undimmed her eye,
Savitri, like a statue, stood,
    Somewhat austere was her reply. (p. 46)

Everyone knows that the deft hand of a true poetic artist is at work. We see a delicacy of touch and a refined sensibility herein. A young woman's fancy is having its play in these lines. Toru is really convincing in her description of feminine charm and beauty as here. The force that we find in Toru's verse is rarely to be seen in the writers of her sex. She depicts the matchless beauty of the goddess Uma thus:

Not weak she seemed, nor delicate,
    Strong was each limb of flexible grace,
And full the bust: the mien elate,
    Like hers, the goddess of the chase
On Latmos,—and oh, the face
    Framed in its cloud of floating hair
No painters hand might hope to trace
    The beauty and the glory there. (p. 94)

And the highest praise that she can bestow on Savitri's charm is this:

The sweet simplicity and grace,
    Abashed the boldest; but the good
God's purity there loved to trace,
    Mirrored in dawning womanhood. (p. 38)

In "Savitri", she upholds the purity of Love and its magical effects. She knows the rapidity of Love—as swift as a lightning flash. She informs us that the 'heart-rose' once opened can never shut. "The Royal Ascetic and the Hindi" is an exquisite study in tenderness of feeling and pathos. In this ballad she administers a gentle rebuke to the stern ascetic author *The Vishnu Purana* who would imply as the concluding moral of his story that for the hermit-king, Bharat, it was a sin to love his nursling. Toru's heart goes out in utter sympathy to the hermit-king, who in direct disregard of the principles of his monastic order—

> Watched and watched
> His favourite through a blinding film of tears
> And could not think of the Beyond at hand:
> So knew he felt the parting.... (p. 105)

Other stories in *Ancient Ballads* are also full of pathetic situations that wring tears from our eyes and move our hearts deeply.

Taking into account the themes employed by Toru in *Ancient Ballads*, it may be said that "Savitri" tells us about the triumph of constancy in love and purity in thought. "Lakshman" demonstrates the unmistakable sense of duty on the part of that prince. "Jogadhya Uma" narrates the sudden appearance of the goddess Uma to a simple pedlar, though not to the ritualistic priest. "The Royal Ascetic and the Hind" relates King Bharat's great asceticism side by side with his growing love for a forlorn fawn. "Dhruva" is about a prince who failed to secure his royal father's love due to his step-mother's meddling and who resolved to attain the coveted spiritual heights. "Buttoo" treats the rejection of a low caste pupil by Dronacharya and the firm resolve of that pupil to excel in the art of magic and archery. "Sindhu" depicts an ideal son in Shravan Kumar, who was devoted to his blind parents wholeheartedly. "Prahlad" is the story of a great devotee of God—Prahlad—who did not hesitate to oppose even his own tyrannical father and, finally, "Sita" highlights that queen's unmerited sufferings at the hands of King Rama.

Miscellaneous Poems

At the end of *Ancient Ballads*, there are seven[35] miscellaneous poems which immediately display Toru's creative power at its best. They are, more or less, personal poems. On her death, they were found among her papers. They represent the whole of her creative period, as the earliest piece was composed during her stay in England (1870-73) and the latest a few months before her untimely death.[36] We shall now take stock of these poems one by one.

"Near Hastings" is the first poem recording an incident in Toru's life in England, she and her ailing sister were taking rest on the beach near Hastings when a lady appeared before them and started talking to them. Before she went away, she offered a few beautiful roses to Aru and thereby won Toru's undying gratitude. Toru did not ask her name or address, but she kept her in her mind's register even long after the lady was gone:

> Her memory will not depart,
> Though grief my years should shade,
> Still bloom her roses in my heart!
> And they shall never fade! (p. 164)

The unusual generosity of that large-hearted lady deeply moved the sensitive poetess. Artistically, the poem is not so fine as some other pieces here, especially "The Lotus" and "Our Casuarina Tree". E.J. Thompson comments on it in a tone of appreciation. He says, '"Near Hastings' is a lyric which brings a lump to the throat, and should convince the most careless and supercilious of the grace and wisdom, the political expediency even, of receiving with kindness these strangers with whom destiny has so strongly linked us and who so often find our manners, like our northern climate, cold."[37] The poem has Toru's characteristic clarity and simplicity of style. It has a lucid diction, as can be seen in the following lines:

> Sweet were the roses,—sweet and full,
> And large as lotus flowers
> That in our own wide tanks we cull
> To deck our Indian bowers. (p. 164)

It is sincere and deeply felt as the poem that follows.

"France-1870", written in a metre strangely irregular, is a little poem which shows Toru's love and admiration for France, which she welcomes as "Head of the human column", while for 'Levite England' she reserves scorn and rebuff. In it the poetess expresses her true sympathy for France during the troublesome days of France-Prussian War. France has been a great nation. If she had been humbled, she would rise again. This is the hope of poetess beautifully expressed in the last stanza of the poem. This inspiring poem has a vigour of expression which makes us easily overlook the ruggedness of its metre:

> Not dead,—oh no,—she cannot die!
> Only a swoon, from loss of blood!
> Levite England passed her by,
> Help Samaritan! None is nigh;
> Who shall stanch me this sanguine blood? (p. 165)

There is "much of passionate feeling"[38] in the poem and when the ear accustoms itself to the strangeness, there is a certain charm about the great irregularity of the rhythm, in which no two verses are alike. There is "an exultant ring"[39] in it.

"The Tree of Life" is an account of a delightful vision that the poetess once had when she lay awake with a sense of weariness with her father's hand in hers. In the silence of the passing moments, there shone, all of a sudden, a strange light stretching itself over a vast plain. In the midst of this illimitable plain, she saw before her eyes:

> A tree with spreading branches and with leaves
> Of divers kinds,—dead silver and live gold,
> Shimmering in radiance that no words may tell!
> (pp. 168-69)

She tells us that she was 'wide awake' and it was 'no dream'. Beside the tree stood an angel, who plucked the leaves and bound them round her head and at their delicious touch the fever in her limbs was gone. She pleads for some to be bound round her father's forehead too and:

> One leaf the Angel took, and therewith touched
> His forehead, and then gently whispered "Nay"!
>
> (p. 169)

She found in the angel's face 'hold pity' and 'love divine'. All at once she opened her tear-dimmed eyes and the light was gone and the angel also disappeared. Only her father lay there patiently reveals the poetess's mystic experience. Biographically, it is of great interest to us as the last poem composed by Toru.

The next poem, "On the Fly-Leaf of Erckmann-chatrian's Novel Entitled *Madame Therese*", records the impression made upon Toru by an incident recorded in the novel, when the French lines were wavering before the Prussian onslaught and the falling standard was marked by a woman, slender, tall and brown and an attack was led by her and a drummer-boy. It is marked by a greater irregularity of rhythm than that found in "France-1870". It is somewhat difficult to determine the metre of the following line:

> Va-nu-pied! When rose high your Marseillaise. (p. 170)

Similarly, to rhyme 'pont' with 'confront' is a case of excess in prosody. The poem decidedly gives us a glimpse of the highly patriotic nature of French.

This poem and "France-1870" have touches of a boldness and imaginative vigour which not appeared before in Toru's work. E.J. Thompson thinks that they misread the political situation then obtaining in France. According to him, "Her (Toru's) love for France was passionate, a second patriotism; but no one today is likely to quarrel with her enthusiasm for the generous nation that has so long and so signally civilization. Her letters show that the France-Prussian War stirred her sympathies: no French-woman could have felt more poignantly for her bleeding country."[40]

The two sonnets, "Baugmaree" and "The Lotus", have been praised by one and all. In the first, the poetess speaks of the scenic beauty of the garden of her family—the garden which girt around with its 'sea of foliage' of varying shades, with its vivid splashed of different colours. It is full of the light-green graceful tamarinds, the mango clumps of deep green colour, the palms standing erect like gray pillars, the seemuls leaning over the quiet pools, the bamboos stretching eastward and the white lotus looking like a cup of silver. In the midst of such natural beauty, one is sure to feel all fresh and cheerful. Toru calls her garden 'a primeval Eden' to be seen only with amazement. The poem displays the poetess's love of nature. In describing the garden, she adopts a simple diction and free rhythm. Mrs. Basu is of opinion that in this poem Toru shows "a native genius".[41] Mr. Thompson says that nothing would be finer or more vivid than the line on the seemuls in blossom in it:

> Red,—red, and startling like a trumpet to sound.
> (p. 171)

The sonnet is distinguished for its startling appositeness of epithets.

"The Lotus" is a quaint story of the birth of that flower. To end the strife as to whether the lily or rose were queen, psyche at last went to Flora and asked for a flower that should be 'delicious as the rose, and stately as the lily in her pride'. And Flora gave the lotus, rose-red and lily-white. The sonnet is so beautiful that it deserves to be quoted in full;

> Love came to Flora asking for a flower.
> That would of flowers be undisputed queen
> The lily and the rose, long, long had been
> Rivals for that high honour. Bards of power
> Had sung their claims. "The rose can never tower
> Like the pale lily with her Juno mien"—
> "But is the lily lovelier?" Thus between
> Flower-factions rang the strife in psyche's bower
> "Give me a flower delicious as the rose
> And stately as the lily in her pride"—
> "But of what colour?"—"Rose-red", Love first chose
> Then prayed,—"No, lily-white,—or, both provide

And Flora gave the lotus, "rose-red" dyed,
And "lily-white", queenliest flower that blows.
(p. 172)

This sonnet and "Our Casuarina Tree" (which follows) have been considered as "beautiful poetic pieces, the outburst of poetic genius".[42] "The Lotus" reveals Toru's "keen sensitiveness to Nature and the responsiveness of her soul to colour".[43] It is like Tennyson's "Akbar's Dream". It shows the poetess's fine command of the sonnet form.

"Our Casuarina Tree" is a really memorable poem. It is an admirable blend of local touché and literary reminiscences, of objective description of the actual tree and the charm of association with Toru's childhood. It opens with an account of the giant tree, festooned with the crimson flowers of a great creeper which wraps it wholly 'like a huge python'. By day and by night it is centre of busy life and sweet bird-song, the finest object on which Toru's eyes rest as she flings wide her window at dawn and something in the early light 'a gray-baboon sits statue-like alone/Watching the sunrise'. The shadow of the tree falls across the tank and makes the white water-lilies look 'like snow enmassed'. Grand and charmingly as the tree is, it is 'dear' chiefly for the memories that cluster round it—memories of a time when happy children played under its shade. The thought brings out an intense yearning towards the playmates now no more:

O sweet companions, loved with love intense,
'For your sakes shall the tree be ever dear!"
Blent with your images, it shall arise
In memory, till the hot tears blind mine eyes! (p. 174)

To the poetess's fancy, the tree in sympathy sounds a dirge-like murmur like 'the breaking on a shingle-beach'. It is the 'eerie speech' or 'lament' of the tree that, she hopes, may perhaps reach 'the unknown land'. Such a wail always strikes a chord of memory in her. Even when she was travelling in France or Italy, it had always sent thought winging its way homeward bringing recollections of the tree dearly loved in childhood. The last stanza of the poem, with its right romantic fervour, unfolds a desire of the poetess for the immortality of verse and ends with the delightful line:

> May Love defend thee from Oblivion's course. (p. 175)

The poem is cast in the eleven-line stanza form, rhyming a b a a, c d d c, e e e. It was really a fresh experiment worthy of Keats and Shelley. Iyengar's opinion on this poem is worth quoting: "In the organization of poem as a whole and in the finish of the individual stanza, in its mastery of phrase and rhythm, in its music of sound and ideas, "Our Casuarina Tree' is a *superb piece* of writing, and gives us a taste of what Toru might have done had not the race of her life been so quickly run."[44] More than being the poetic evocation of the tree, the poem is a meeting-point for the past and the present, for time and eternity.

The critical world had received this poem with open arms. E.J. Thompson considers it as "the most remarkable poem ever written in English by a foreigner, shows her already possessed of mastery over the more elaborate and architectural forms of verse".[45] Harihar Das remarks thus about it: "For its rich imagery, the music of its verse, and the tenderness and pathos with which it is instinct, we would place this poem second to none in the volume."[46] Mukerjea thinks that it is "one of the great architectural pieces in English poetry".[47] And Lotika Basu, too, is all praise for the "riper perfection"[48] attained in this piece. Obviously, the poem "our Casuarina Tree" stands out for its sweet music and perfect texture. The poetic diction is free of all unnecessary twists or twangs herein. Not even a single critic has spoken a word against it. No doubt, it is Toru's superb creation in poetic world.

NOTES

1. A.N. Dwivedi, "Toru Dutt and Her Poetry", *World Literature Written in English,* 14, No. 2 (Nov. 1975), 286.
2. K.R.S. Iyenger, *Indian Writing in English,* p. 64.

3. A.N. Dwivedi, ed. *Ancient Ballads and Legends of Hindustan* (Bareilly: Prakash Book Depot, 1976), p. 63.
4. Harihar Das, *op. cit.*, p. 331.
5. E. Gosse, "Introductory Memoir", *Ancient Ballads*. pp. xxii-iii.
6. Harihar Das, "The Classical Tradition in Toru Dutt's Poetry", *Asiatic Review* (October 1931), pp. 695-96.
7. T.O.D. *The Bengali Writers of English Verse* (1918), p. 22.
8. B.K. Talookdar, "The Poetry of Toru Dutt," *Journal of the University of Bombay* (1936), p. 82.
9. Amaranatha Jha, "Introductory Memoir", *Ancient Ballads,* p. 30.
10. Radhakamal Mukerjee et al., "Writers and Social Reformers: Great Indian Women of the Nineteenth Century", *Great Women of India* (1953), p. 402.
11. Alokerjan Dasgupta, "The Fragile Exotic Blossom of Songs", *Indian Literature,* IX, No. 2 (1966), 11.
12. K.R.S. Iyenger, *Indian Writing in English* (1973), pp. 65-66.
13. Padmini Sengupta, *Toru Dutt* (1968), p. 82.
14. P.C. Kotoky, *Indo-English Poetry* (1969), p. 8.
15. Harihar Das, "The Classical Tradition in Toru Dutt's Poetry", *Asiatic Review,* p. 700.
16. Toru Dutt, *Ancient Ballads and Legends of Hindustan,* ed. Amaranatha Jha (Allahabad: Kitabistan, 1969), p. 38. (All subsequent quotations from *Ancient Ballads* refer to this edition.)
17. H. Das, "The Classical Tradition in Toru Dutt's Poetry", *Asiatic Review*, p. 703.
18. *Ibid.*, p. 704.
19. Harihar Das, *The Life and Litters of Toru Dutt,* p. 333.
20. *Idem.*
21. Lotika Basu incorrectly imagines that the story is taken from the *Purans. Indian Writers of English Verse* (Calcutta: The Univ. Press, 1933), p. 77.
22. Lotika Basu, *op. cit.*, p. 77.
23. Harihar Das, "The Classical Tradition in Toru Dutt's Poetry", *Asiatic Review*, p. 700.
24. *Idem.*
25. P.C. Kotoky, *Indo-English Poetry*, p. 23.
26. S.V. Mukerjea, *Disjects Membra* (Bangalore: The Indian Institute of World Culture, 1959), p. 60.

27. Harihar Das, "The Classical Tradition in Toru Dutt's Poetry", *Asiatic Review,* p. 710.
28. P.C. Kotoky, *Indo-English Poetry,* pp. 24-25.
29. R. Sethusavithri, "Indian Writers of English: (I) Toru Dutt", *The Literary Criterion,* 3 (Winter 1953), 40.
30. Harihar Das, "The Classical Tradition in Toru Dutt Poetry", *Asiatic Review,* p. 714.
31. E.J. Thompson, "Supplementary Review", *The Life and Letters of Toru Dutt,* p. 343.
32. *Idem.*
33. Edmund Gosse, "Introductory Memoir', *Ancient Ballads and Legends of Hindustan,* p. xxiv.
34. A.N. Dwivedi, "Toru Dutt and Her Poetry", *WLWE* (U.S.A.), 14, No. 2 (Nov. 1975), p. 287.
35. Lotika Basu erroneously thinks that the number of these poems is 'five or six—See her *Indian Writters of English Verse,* p. 78.
36. B.K. Talookdar, "The Poetry of Toru Dutt", *Journal of the University of Bombay,* IV, Part 6. p. 88.
37. E.J. Thompson, "Supplementary Review", *The Life and Letters of Toru Dutt,* ed. Harihar Das, p. 344.
38. Harihar Das, *The Life and Letters of Toru Dutt,* p. 338.
39. S.V. Mukerjea, *Disjecta Membra,* p. 54.
40. E.J. Thompson, "Supplementary Review", *The Life and Letters of Toru Dutt,* ed. Harihar Das, p. 344.
41. Lotika Basu, *Indian Writers of English Verse,* p. 79.
42. Jyotis Chandra Das Gupta, "Toru Dutt", *National Biography for India,* IV, p. 304.
43. Izzat Yar Khan, "Toru Dutt—Nineteenth Century Indian Songbird," *The Statesman* (March 14, 1954), n.p.
44. K.R.S. Iyengar, *Indian Writing in English,* p. 73.
45. E.J. Thompson, "Supplementary Review", *The Life and Letters of Toru Dutt,* pp. 342-43.
46. Harihar Das, *op. cit.,* p. 341.
47. S.V. Mukerjea, *Disjecta Merbra,* p. 53. R. Sethusavitri's article in *The Literary Criterion,* 3 (Winter 1953), p. 40.
48. Lotika Basu, *Indian Writers of English Verse,* p. 80.

Mind and Art of Toru Dutt

6

The Development of Her Poetic Art and Vision

Perfection is the most desired ideal in art. It does not come in the twinkling of an eye; instead, it is a matter of constant application and growth. The moment an artist ceases to apply himself wholeheartedly to his work and to 'grow regularly' his art becomes stale and imperfect. Toru Dutt is a poetic artist who applies herself to her art sincerely and tries to 'grow' from within ceaselessly. It is the desire of application and growth that is so conspicuous in her art. It is this desire that makes her restless to experiment with a number of themes and verse-forms. It is this that explains the great dynamism and substantiality of her poetry.

But the development of art and vision comes with the growth of years. It requires a hard practice, an unflagging fancy and a mature mind. The reader of Toru Dutt knows that her early poetry suffers from certain shortcomings of metre, rhythm and grammar, but they disappear with the greater maturity of her mind. The *Sheaf* has many inversions, archaic words and phrases and twisted expressions and also a discordant music here and there, as pointed out by the reviewers of *The Examiner* and *The Englishman*, but the same cannot be said of *Ancient Ballads* and miscellaneous poems. If the *Sheaf* holds out a promise for an upcoming poetess, *Ancient Ballads* is, in a way, the fulfillment of that promise. This naturally leads us to construe that Toru Dutt's art constantly grew and was on trial until it gained in scope and depth towards the close of her life on earth.

Diction

The diction that one comes across in Toru's poetry is usually simple clear and sweet, though this is not literally true in case of some of translations. Here is an example of her sweet diction:

> What was the meaning—was it love?
> Love at first sight, as poets sing,
> Is then no fiction?[1] (p. 40)

And this is an illustration of her obtuse diction to be found in some of her translations:

> Dante, old Gibelin! When I see only in passing
> The plaster white and dull of this mask so puissant
> That Art has bequeathed us of thy features majestic,
> I cannot help feeling a slight shudder O poet;
> So strongly the band of genius and that of misfortune
> Have imprinted upon them the dark seal of sorrow.[2]
> (p. 177)

But here, Toru is not her usual self. In many of her translations she writes with a force that seems to come from within her. In this connection, one may cite "To Those Who Sleep" by Victor Hugo:

> Lo; He lifts up His hand,
> And the tigers fly howling through deserts of sand,
> And the sea-serpents crawl
> Obedient and meek; He breathes on idols of gold
> In their temples of marble gigantic and old
> And like Dagon they zall:
>
> You are not armed? It matters not,
> Tear out the hinges of the door!
> A hammer has deliverance wrought:
> David had pebbles from the shore, (p. 87)

As an Indo-Anglian author, Toru's main achievement lies in her effective mastery of the medium. She shows in her poetry a fine sense of the English language, a feeling for its rhythm and diction. So remarkable is her treatment of diction and rhythm that she was regarded by many as an Englishman writing under the pseudonym of 'Toru Dutt'. There is an elasticity in her verse which renders it graceful and interesting. The variance of diction according to the need of the occasion may be easily found in it; she has, thus, used monosyllabic as well as polysyllabic diction with much success. As an instance of the first variety, we may take up the following from "Sindhu":

> Ah me! What means this?—Hark, a cry,
> A feeble human wail,
> "Oh God!" it said—"I die,—I die,
> Who'll carry home the pail?" (p. 131)

And for the second variety, the following from "Dhruva" may be quoted:

> Mother, thy words of consolation find
> Nor resting-place, nor echo in this heart
> Broken by words, severe, repulsing Love
> That timidly approached to worship. (p. 111)

One really marvels at the vast resourcefulness of Toru's diction. Of course, there are archaisms, inversions, twistings at places which partly mar the overall effect of her art. Toru does not hesitate to employ even French words and expressions in her poetry: for example, "Va-nu-pieds!" in the poem "On the Fly-Leaf of Erckmann-Chatrian's Novel Entitled *Madame Therese*". It must be admitted that she is not conversant with the colloquial turns of modern English.[3]

Rhythm

As in the case of diction, Toru's rhythm has received a mixed reaction from critics. It is true that she sometimes succeeds and sometimes fails in capturing the English tunes.

There is, no doubt, much force and fire in Toru's verse and lyricism touches a high-watermark at times, such as in:

The doors of every house are hung
With gay festoons of leaves and flowers;
And blazing banners broad are flung,
And trumpets blown from castle towers. (p. 49)

And in:

Past all the houses, past the walls,
Past gardens gay, and hedgerows trim,
Past fields, where sinuous brooklets small
With mother silver to me trim
Glance in the sun's expiring light,
Past frowning hills, past pastures wild,
At last arises on the sight,
Foliage on foliage densely piled. (p. 49)

In the latter passage, the repetitive use of 'past' and 'I', 'g' and 'd' sounds produce a charming rhythm. Toru was at home in the handing of ballads and sonnets and the reader feels delighted to read them. They are also free from the burdensomeness and dullness of her blank verse. What actually Toru lacked was "mellow sweetness' to perfect her as an English poet, "of no other oriental who has ever lived can the same be said".[4] Speaking of her melodies, Anant says that they "were often foreign if not harsh to the English ear" and that they were "the melodies of Bengal, her native land, the melodies which she drank in so often that they now formed part of her very soul".[5] Her lapses in rhythm can be easily traced in the *Sheaf*, at least in some of her renderings, such as in:

They are the watch-dogs, terrible, superb,
Enormous, faithfully that Paris guard.
As at each moment we could be surprised,

As at wild horde is there, as ambush vile
Creeps sometimes even to the city walls.
(*The Forts of Paris*, p. 137)

Nothing to speak of rhyme, there is hardly rhythm in this extract. Milton produced sonorous and haunting music in his blank verse, but that is totally lacking here.

Versification

On the appearance of the *Sheaf*, Toru's versification was found to be 'crude' and 'wooden'. This is how *The Englishman* greeted it: "Miss Dutt's metre often limps, her grammar is not always faultless, and her expressions are sometimes quaint or tame". Mr. Gosse also pointed out that at times "the rules of our prosody are absolutely ignored". Dr. Edward J. Thompson remarks as follow:

> It is easy to feel that, in the work done, she never escaped from the influence of her favourite English poets, such writers as Mrs. Browning, whose work did not furnish satisfactory prosodic models. The metres used by Toru Dutt are nearly always of the simplest, and her use of them is marred by much crudity. Yet against this must be set the many sings of haste and lack of opportunity to finish. The punctuation of the *Ballads*, for example, is chaotic.... Yet, even amid the many marks of immaturity and haste, there are signs that she would have escaped before long from many of her prosodic limitations. "Our Casuarina Tree", surely the most remarkable poem ever written in English by a foreigner, shows her already possessed of mastery over the more elaborate and architectural form of verse. In any case, there is enough to show that experience and practice would have brought release from the cramping and elementary forms that she used....[6]

As contrasted to this, Sri Aurobindo has observed: "Toru Dutt was an accomplished verse-builder with a delicate-talent and some outbreaks of genius and she wrote things that were attractive and sometimes something that had a strong energy of language and a rhymic force".[7] Elsewhere he is said to have remarkable that "she has written poetry not as an Indian writing in English but like an English woman".[8] E.F. Oaten, appreciating Toru's real creative and imaginative power, has taken note of her 'almost faultless technical skill'.

Coming to the *Sheaf*, we find "the metre at least is smooth and suggestive of no labour or hard toil in its making".[9] Such, for instance, is Berat's "My Normandy" or Peyrat's "Roland". This is the last stanza of "My Normandy":

> There is an age, alas! In life,
>   'When every idle dream must end,
> An age of introspection, rife
>   With memories that cross and blend.
> When such an age arrives for me,
>   And folds her wing, my muse, to rest,
> May I behold my Normandy,
>   The favoured land I love the best. (p. 36)

Here one finds the same kind of smooth rhythm and rhyme as in Aru's rendering of "Morning Serenade", which has been oft praised by critics.

As hinted earlier, Toru tried her hand at blank verse too, but not very successfully. In a note to a piece by Louis Bouihet, she says: "Although a Frenchman would faint away at the idea of blank verse, which is not allowed in French poetry, we have not hesitated to render this piece in that form, as well as others".[10] Her lines are all end-stopped and she is never really happy in blank verse, though a few lines in "The Death of the Wolf" and some in the *Ancient Ballads*, especially "The Royal Ascetic and the Hind", "Dhruva" and "Sita", lead us to believe that with more practice she would have been just as much at home in that form as in so many others, notably the sonnet.

Toru seems to have had a great liking for the sonnet form. In *Ancient Ballads*, we have two charming sonnets—"Sonnet-Baugmaree" and "Sonnet—The Lotus". Her biographer, Harihar Das is aware of her partiality to this form. In the *Sheaf*, there is an original sonnet addressed to the father—one entitled "A mon Pere".

This *Sheaf* is curiously uneven in merit. There are poems in it when read like bad prose translations, their closeness to the original being their sole worth, but there are others which are real products of genius.

Some distinct verse-forms in *Ancient Ballads* are: the ballad, the blank verse (of which we have already spoken and the octolined stanzas. Toru used the first form in "Savitri", "Jogadhya Uma" and "Sindhu" and the last in "Lakshman", "Buttoo" and "Prahlad". She, however, is at her best in handling the ballad-form. Only one example is being given below to consolidate the statement:

> I know in such a world as this
> No one can gain his heart's desire,
> Or pass the years in perfect bliss;
> Like gold we must be tried by fire. (p. 67)

In this quatrain, sense glides along without interruptions. It has a wonderful metrical felicity.

Narration and Description

The narrative and descriptive powers of Toru Dutt are best seen in *Ancient Ballads*. She had a rare gift of story-telling, of arousing interest and curiosity, of creative suspense and of drawing character. It may be reasonably said, remarks Dr. Jha, that "had she lived longer she would have attained distinction in narrative verse and in descriptive verse".[11] Toru's narrative skill is beautifully manifested in the way she manages to tell the stories of the past—of Savitri, Sita, Jogadhya Uma, Lakshman, Buttoo, Sindhu, Prahlad, Bharat and Dhruva. But perhaps in descriptive poetry she is even superior. This is how Yama, the God of Death, is described:

> Upon his head he wore a crown
> That shimmered in the doubtful light;

His vestment scarlet reached low down.
His waist, a golden girdle dight.
His skin was dark as bronze: his face
Irradiate, and yet sever;
His eyes had much of love and grace,
But glowed so bright, they filled with fear. (p. 63)

Toru described Savitri's faint hopes and vivid fears and later her bold encounter with Yama after the death of Satyavan with immaculate skill.

Minute Observation of Nature

Toru's deep love of Nature and her keen appreciation of natural beautiful are visible in all her productions. The *Champak* and the lotus and the *Kokila* always inspired her song and made her ecstatical. In the presence of natural beauty her heart leapt up with an unspeakable delight and her lips, like Keats's, quivered in a state of rapture. Here is a beautiful description of the sunset on an Indian lake to be found in "Sindhu":

Upon the glassy surface fell
The lest beams of the day,
Like fiery darts, that lengthening swell,
As breezes wake and play.

Osiers and willows on the edge
And purple buds and red,
Leant down,—and, mid the pale greens edge
The lotus raised its head.

And softly, softly, hour by hour
Light faded, and a veil
Fell over tree, and wave, and flower,
On came the twilight pale. (pp. 129-30)

As one reads the ballads, one is struck with the large space covered by descriptions of Nature; for example:

What glorious trees! The somber saul
On which the eye delights to rest,
The betel-nut,—a pillar tall,
With feathery branches for a crest,
The light-leaved tamarind spreading wide,
The pale faint-scented bitter neem,
The seemul, gorgeous as a bride,
With flowers that have the ruby's gleam,
The Indian fig's pavilion tent
In which whole armies might repose,
With here and there a little rent,
The sunset's beauty to disclose,
The bamboo bough that sway and swing
'Neath bulbuls as the south wind blows,
The mango-tope, a close dark ring,
Home of the rooks and clamorous crows,

The champak, bok, and South-Sea pine,
The nagessur with pendant flowers
Like ear-rings,—and the forest vine
That clinging over all, empowers,
The sirish famed in sanscrit song,
Which rural maidens love to wear,
The peepul giant-like and strong,
The bramble with its matter hair,

All these; and thousands, thousands more,
With helmet red, or golden crown,
Or green tiara, rose before
The youth in evening's shadows brown.

("Buttoo", pp. 115-16)

What is quoted here is actually a part of a very long yet charming description of Nature. It is not that the *Sheaf* has no such descriptions and this is a pen-picture of the fall of the leaves in the autumn season:

The autumn had bestrewed the vale
With withered leaves,—the woods were left
Bare, and of mystery bereft,
And voiceless was the nightingale;
Sad, almost dying in his dawn,
A sick youth, wandered slow, in tears,
Once more in places far withdrawn
That he had loved in earlier years. (p. 126)

This passage shows that not only the lovely pictures of Nature drew Toru's attention but also the naked and deserted ones and she gave room to both of them in her poetry.

Imagery and Symbol

Toru has sometimes made a fine use of images and symbols in her poetry. It is to be seen in *Ancient Ballads*. Her imagery is often drawn with a masculine vigour and boldness. Though a frail woman herself, she displayed a wonderful power in grappling with the sublime and the terrible. Thus, Savitri has:

My daughter, night with ebon wing
Hovers above: the hour is late. (p. 56)

Here the darkness of the night is compared to the black skin of an ebony. Another beautiful image is to be found in the following:

She took the soul,
No bigger than the human thumb. (p. 74)

In it an abstract thing has been measured in terms of a concrete thing. This is yet another impressive image in "Savitri":

I had a pain, as if an asp
Gnawed in my brain. (p. 74)

The image of a gnawing 'asp' has been evoked herein to express the intensity of pain. The following passage is also very effective in covering a vivid imagery:

The shaven stalks of grass,
Kusha and kasha, by its new teeth clipped,
Remind me of it, as they stand in lines
Like pious boys who chant the Sa, ga Veda
Shorn by their vows of all their wealth of hair. (p. 104)

The 'shaven stalks of grass' look like some hairless *brahmacharis* and this is really a masterialy stroke of Toru's fertile imagination.

We don't find a systematic network of symbolism in Toru's poetry. Only very rarely has she used symbols. Thus, in "Savitri", the night and its shades are associated with death and distress: in "The Tree of Life", the "tree" becomes a symbol of life and the 'Angel' of Jesus Christ; and "Our Casuarina Tree" is more than the poetic evocation of a tree,—it is rather recapturing the past and immortalising the moments of time so recaptured. In the words of Dr. Iyengar, "The tree is both tree and symbol, and in it are implicated both time and eternity".[12]

Figures of Speech

Figures of speech are generally used to adorn the language and to convey ideas more effectively than in the normal course. Now, Toru has employed them for both purposes.

The figures of speech which Toru has frequently used are simile metaphor, onomatopoeia, personification, alliteration and hyperbole. Instances of simile in *Ancient Ballads* are: 'When glided like a music-strain Savitri's presence through the room' (p. 43); 'Nor melt his linege like the frost' (p. 45); 'Tall tree like pillar's (p. 51); 'It came as chainless as the wind' (p. 58); 'He staggers, like a sleepy child' (p. 59); 'His skin was dark as bronze' (p. 63); 'The dreadful sword/Like lightning glanced one moment dire' (p. 64); 'They lacerate my inmost heart/And torture me, like poisioned swords' (p. 87); 'the lion roar...like a thunder-clap/Burst in that solitude from a thicket high' (p. 102); 'Unseen the magic arrow came...like lightning flame/Sudden and sharp' (p. 114) and 'The water-lilies spring, like snow enmassed' (p. 174). Instances of metaphor in it are:

'His merit still remains a star' (p. 45); 'The pair look statues, magic-bound' (p. 60); Savitri 'looked the goddess of the land' (p. 62), etc. One beautiful instance of onomatopoeia is:

> But the good
> God's purity there loved to trace,
> Mirrored in dawning womanhood. (p. 38)

The frequency of 'd' sound in it gives a sense of holy fear in God-fearing view. Another instance is: 'Whizzing the deadly arrow flew/Ear-guided, on the game' (p. 131). A fine example of personification is:

> Rang trump, and conch, and piercing fife,
> Woke Echo from her bed!
> The solemn woods with sounds were rife
> As on the pageant sped. (p. 127)

Instances of alliteration are: 'Stern warriors, when they saw her, smiled, /As mountains smile to see the spring' (p. 37); 'A stately sable warrior sprang' (p. 156), etc. Examples of hyperbole are: 'All these, and thousands, thousands more...rose before/ The youth in evening is shadows brown' (p. 116); 'Hundreds, nay thousands, on they went' (p. 127), etc.

The *Sheaf* is also not without these figures of speech, but for Toru's original contribution to these areas of literary grace one will have to go to *Ancient Ballads.*

Autobiographical Touches in Her Poetry

Toru was a reserved woman and she rarely resorted to airing out personal feeling in her verse, but it does not mean that her verse is totally devoid of personal touches. Both of her poetical volumes contain beautiful autobiographical flashes. Thus, in the *Sheaf*, we have "My Vocation" and "The Death of a Young Girl", among others. This is how Toru writes in the former:

All men have a task,
    And to sing is my lot—
No meed from men I ask
    But one kindly thought,
My vocation is high—
    'Mid the glasses that sing,
Still—still comes that reply,
    Chant poor little thing. (pp. 10-11)

Here she hints at her vocation as a poetess. In the latter, we have the following:

She died in earliest womanhood;
    Thus dies, and leaves behind no trace,
A bird's song in a leafy wood—
    Thus melts a sweet smile from a face. (p. 35)

This entire poem is applicable to the poetess's sister, Aru, who died at the age of twenty, leaving behind no trace of herself.

Ancient Ballads has also some poems in which the personal note is clearly articulated. Of such poems, mention may be made of "Jogadhya Uma", "Sita" and Miscellaneous poems (almost all). At the end of "Jogadhya Uma", Toru gives us this stanza:

Absurd may be the tale I tell,
    Ill-suited to the marching time,
I loved the lips from which it fell,
    So let it stand among my rhymes. (p. 100)

In it she forwards the reason for her love of this story. "Sita" is also autobiographical in content. The 'three happy children in a darkened room' are none else but Abju, Aru and Toru, who used to gather in the evening by the side of fire and the mother used to narrate the pathetic tale of Sita to them, they were deeply moved. Among the Miscellaneous poems,

"Near Hastings", "The Tree of Life", the two sonnets and "Our Casuarina Tree" are distinctly autobiographical in detail and in execution. In the last-named poem, we have:

> But not because of its magnificence
>   Dear is the Casuarina to my soul;
> Beneath it we have played; though years may roll,
>   O sweet companions, loved with love intense,
> For your sakes shall the tree be ever dear! (p. 174)

It is reminiscent of the poetess's girlhood and the 'sweet companions' with whom she then played. By the way, the glimpses of the poetess's personal life may be best had in her letters.

Themes

The subject that attracted Toru Dutt most were pathetic. There are scores of poems in the *Sheaf* to confirm it. "The Young Captive", "The Emigration of Pleasure", "The Lost Path", "Romance of Nina", "Morning Serenade", "The Death of a Young Girl", "The Captive to the Wallows" and many others are full of pathos and tender feelings. The captives, the vanquished and the sufferers easily caught her attention and moved her to write. Seldom does she speak about Love and when she does so, it is invariably pure and sublime. Patriotic themes were no less dearer to her. Her ballads are couched in patriotic instincts and native traditions. The stories of the past evoked a sympathetic response from her. Of all the themes, the French war against the Prussians touched her profoundly. Her two poems, "French 1870" and "On the Fly-Leaf of Erckmann-Chatrain's Novel Entitled *Madame Therese*", celebrate it in a grand manner. *Ancient Ballads* shows that for her themes Toru usually drew upon the *Ramayana*, the *Mahabharata*, the *Vishnu Purana* and the folklore (as in case of "Jogadhya Uma"). Like Shakespeare, Toru shows little originality in inventing new themes for her poetry; her real originality lies in the way she executes them. That is also the considered opinion of Mr. Vaish when he remarks: "Toru was less original in themes but she was original in versifying them".[13]

Technical Excellences

The delicacy and lightness of touch displayed in Toru's verse bear testimony to her faultless and refined poetic taste and the music of her poetry is not the least negligible feature of her work. There is abundant simplicity and spontaneity in her verse.

If in the *Sheaf* Toru found vocation as well as her voice, in *Ancient Ballads* she attained technical virtues which may do credit to any modern poet. In the latter, she managed the octosyllabic line with considerable dexterity; her rhymes are rarely far-fetched and the sense glides alone without interruptions. In connection with her 'wooden' blank verse, it is to be noted that it yields its peculiar charm only to the lucky few like Christopher Marlowe, John Milton and William Shakespeare. A few more years could have perfected the form and is likely that she might have written a powerful sonnet-sequence or poetic tragedy in the age of her maturity.[14]

Speaking of the technical character of *Ancient Ballads*, Sir Gosse suggests that in spite of much in it that is "rough and incholate", it shows that "Toru was advancing in her mastery of English verse".[15] There is, therefore, no need to plead for indulgence in the critical in the estimate of Toru's poetical works. Her poetical treasure is too valuable to sink into oblivion and she has exhibited, within its short compass, many of the essential virtues, including the technical ones, of a genuine poet.

NOTES

1. The textual quotations that follow in this chapter are from Dr. Jha's edition of *Ancient Ballads*, p. 40.
2. The textual quotations that follow in this chapter are from the second edition of *A Sheaf*.
3. Edmund Gosse, "Introductory Memories", *Ancient Ballads*, p. xxv.
4. *Ibid.*, p. xxvii.
5. Anant, "Gifted Poetess", *The Times of India*, March 7, 1954.

6. E.J. Thompson, "Supplementary Review", *The Life and Letters of Toru Dutt,* pp. 342-43.
7. Shri Aurobindo, *Letters* (Third Series), p. 245.
8. A.B. Purani, *Evening Talks with Sri Aurobindo* (First Series, 1959), p. 283.
9. B.K. Talookar, "The Poetry of Toru Dutt", *Journal of the University of Bombay,* IV, part 6, 77.
10. Toru Dutt, "Notes", *A Sheaf*, p. 267.
11. Amaranatha Jha, "Introductory Memoir", *Ancient Ballads*, p. 30.
12. K.R. Srinivasa Iyengar, *Indian Writing in English*, p. 72.
13. Y.N. Vaish, "Toru Dutt", *The Modern Review* (December 1966), p. 437.
14. Mr. Iyengar's *Indian Contribution to English Literature,* p. 20.
15. Edmund Gosse, "Introductory Memoir", *Ancient Ballads*, p. xxix.

Cultural Sensibility in the Poetry of Toru Dutt

7

Toru's Outlook Upon Life

Toru's outlook upon life had been pessimistic and gloomy. The main reason for this outlook was that she saw a number of tragedies at home and that she herself hardly enjoyed a sound health. Toru's only brother, Abju, died in 1865 at an early age, plunging the entire family into misery and disappointment. Thereafter, her beloved sister, Aru, an adept in poetry and painting, died of consumption in 1874. This made the sensitive poetess sad and companionless. On the death of Aru, she wrote to her dear friend, Mary Martin, as follows: "The Lord has taken dear Aru from us. It is a sore trial for us, but His will be done. We know that he doeth all things for our good."[1] By and by, Toru's own health ran down owing to recurrent attacks of fever and cough spasms; she spat a great deal of blood, which left her 'quite weak and prostrate'. She was compelled to keep within doors and even writing letters was an effort she could not stand. It is a harrowing tale indeed. How could a girl constantly attacked by disease and suffering be of optimistic nature or paint the comic and the sunny sides of life in her work?

Toru's poetical compositions bear out the above statement. In both *A Sheaf* and *Ancient Ballads* there are so many poems dealing with the buffets and sorrows of life, with deaths and diseases, with lost hopes and suppressed feelings. The captives and the prisoners, the downtrodden and the poor also attracted Toru's attention and there are certain poems on theses themes, too. In the *Sheaf*, we have poems like "The Peasant's Dilemma", "The Young Captive", "The Emigration of Pleasure", "My Vocation", "The Young Girl", "The Lost Path", "Morning

Serenade", "The Death of a Young Girl", "The Captive to the Swallow", "Sonnet—The Broken Bell", "Loneliness", "Oh Desert of the Heart", "The Rose and the Tomb", "The Political Prisoner", "The Death of the Wolf", "Sonnet—A Dream", "The Death of a Daughter", "Sonnet—Isolation" and "The Tears of Racine", which are all on unhappy and none-too-fresh conditions of life. Of these, "The Young Captive" is to be marked out for its deep pathetic feelings. In it the captive says thus:

> Oh Death, thou canst wait; leave, leave me to dream,
> And strike at the hearts when Despair is supreme,
>   And shame hails thy dart as a boon!
> For me Dales has arbours unknown to the throngs,
> The world has delights, the Muses have songs,
>   I wish not to perish too soon. (*A Sheaf*, p. 4)

And further:

> A prisoner myself broken-hearted and crushed,
> From my heart to my lips all my sympathies rushed,
>   And my lyre from its slumbers awoke;
> At these sorrows, these wishes, of a captive, I heard,
> And to rhyme and to measure I married each word
>   As softly and simply she spoke. (p. 5)

The poem "My Vocation" is profoundly touching. It carries an intense personal tone. Only the first stanza is being given here to substantiate the point:

> A waif on this earth,
>   Sick, ugly and small,
> Contemned from my birth,
>   And rejected by all,
> From my lips broke a cry,
>   Such as anguish may wring,
> Sing,—said God in reply,
>   Chant poor little thing. (p. 10)

The lonely life of the poetess on this earth and her sickness and smallness are nicely pictured in it. Instances like this can be multiplied and we shall give one more here before we pass on to examine the trends of thought in Toru's poetry. This time we are taking up "The Death of a Daughter", which runs as follows:

Oh, I was wild like a mad man at first,
Three days I wept bitter tears and accurst;
O those whom God of your hope hath bereft!
Fathers and mothers like me lonely left!
Have ye felt what I felt; and known it all?
And longed to dash your heads on the wall?
Have you been like me in open revolt,
And defied the Hand that had hurled the bolt?

Does God permit such misfortune, nor care
That our souls be filled with utter despair?
It seemed as the whole were a frightful dream,
She could not have left me thus like a fleam;
Ha! That is her laughter in the next room!
Oh no, she cannot be dead in the tomb,
There shall he enter,—come here by this door,
And her step shall be music to me as before.

Oh! How oft have I said,—silence,—she speaks,
Hold,—'tis her hand on the key, and it creaks,
Wait—she comes!—I must hear,—leave me,—go out,
For she is in this mansion, somewhere without doubt.
(pp. 180-81)

It is heart-rending poem; the father is unable to sustain the loss of his daughter. A good number of poems that Toru selected for her translation from the original French are actually of the same nature, having intensity of emotion and tenderness of feeling.

In *Ancient Ballads*, the narratives are charged with lyric effusion of joy and pathos, anger and sorrow. As in her translations from the French poets, Toru has shown her inclination towards some pathetic and sorry incidents of life in the majority of her longer poems. Thus, "Savitri" brings to light the untimely death of Satyavan and the bold encounter of Savitri with the God of Death: "Lakshman" the taunts and hot words of Sita for a devoted worker; "The Royal Ascetic and the Hind" the failure of a great king as an ascetic; "Dhruva" the disappointment of that Prince and his leaving the palace for the higher values of life; "Buttoo" the sad incident of thumb-severing in deference to the wishes of a renowned teacher; "Sindhu" the painful death of Sharavan Kumar in the service of his old and blind parents; and "Sita" the underserved sufferings of that queen in the forest after having been exiled from Ayodhya by Rama. This is how Toru pictures Sita rebuking and taunting Lakshman:

> He perishes—well, let him die!
>   His wife henceforth shall be mine own!
> Can that thought deep imbedded lie
>   Within thy heart's most secret zone!
> Search well and see! One brother takes
>   His kingdom,—one would take his wife!
> A fair partition!—But it makes
>   Me shudder, and abhor my life.
>
> ("Lakshman", p. 85)

From every line of this passage anger and scorn leap up and it is not difficult to deduce that Sita is not her usual self. The most moving lines in the whole of *Ancient Ballads* are the following from "Sita":

> But who is this fair lady! Not in vain
> She weeps,—for lo! At every tear she sheds
> Tears from three pairs of young eyes fall amain,
> And bowed in sorrow are the three young hands.
>
> (p. 158)

In them we find a deep sense of pathos. The autobiographical touch is also unmistakable in them. Taking the poems so far discussed into account, we can safely say that the notes of frustration and longing are predominant in Toru's poetry and that suffering and gloom caused by ill-health were her shadow-companions. Toru, no doubt, waged a heroic fight against odds, but had finally to succumb to the foul desease.

Christian Thought

It is well-known fact that Toru Dutt was a devout Christian. Her father, along with many other prominent members of the Dutt family accepted Christianity drifted away from Hinduism. This was a matter of discontentment between Toru's parents, the mother being a devout Hindu lady. Later on she adjusted to the changed circumstance and translated from English into Bengali a book, *The Blood of Jesus*, which was published by Tract and Book Society of Calcutta. Her philanthropy was well-known and after her death in 1900 she left a handsome contribution towards the building of the Oxford Mission Church at Barisal, one of the finest in Bengal.

At the critical moment of the family, Mr. Govin Chunder wrote a touching poem called "The Hindu Convert to His Wife", an extract of which is quoted below:

> It was not thus, in former hours,
>   We parted or we met;
> It was not thus, when Love's young flowers
>   With hope and joy were wet.
> That kindling cheek, overted eye,
> That heaving breast and stifled sigh,
>   Attest thy feeling yet.
> It was not thus, reserved and cold,
> Like strangers, that we met of old.[2]

Persuasions of this kind had good effect on Mrs. Dutt, as we have already noted. Many of the poems by Mr. Dutt collected in *The Dutt Family Album* (1870) are mostly didactic in character and deal with the mysteries of birth and the after life, written from the Christian point of view.

Born in such a family, Toru Dutt, as well as other children of Mr. Dutt, made the *Bible* a main support of her tormented life. She had full faith in God, Christ and the Holy Spirit. She was a regular goer to the Church and played "a small harmonium"[3] there. In one of her letters, she told Mary Martin, "We go to the Old Church on every Sunday; it is very far from our house, that is the only inconvenience".[4] She also told Miss Martin with sadness that her grandmother was "still a Hindu".[5] On her death, her funeral rites were performed according to Christian traditions, she was buried in the M.S. Cemetery in the Upper Circular Road, Calcutta and on her tombstone appeared the following inscription:

TORU DUTT
YOUNGEST DAUGHTER OF
GOVIN CHUNDER DUTT,
Born 4 March, 1856,
Died 30th August, 1877.
Be thou faithful unto Death and I
will give thee a crown of life.
Rev. II. 10.

These details are given here to show that Toru was reared in a Hindu family which later shifted its loyalty to Christianity and that Toru remained a faithful Christian throughout her life after the conversion.

As regards her poetry, *A Sheaf* is not to be supposed to contain anything that has a direct bearing upon Toru's religion and beliefs, for it is merely a collection of translated poems, which generally reflect the attitude and the faith of the respective original French authors and not of the translator. Even if we suppose that Toru was a translator who took sufficient liberty in rendering the poems, we can't infer in any way that the beliefs conveyed in them are her own. She, no doubt, took liberty in translating the pieces, but that is mostly confined to the choice of certain words, phrases and expressions.

She never tried, as a translator, to spoil or distort the very essence of the originals and therein lies her credit.

In *Ancient Ballads*, which is soaked in Indian myths and legends and which is essentially Indian in temper and treatment, there are only a few hints at Christian belief and thought and they, too, may be taken to be somewhat far-fetched. However, in, "The Royal Ascetic and the Hind", there is "a pronouncedly Christian note"[6] in the comments of Toru Dutt on the failure of Bharat as an ascetic. In fact, she wrongly thinks that it is implied in the original that by yielding to the love of a forlorn fawn Bharat had failed in his *Yoga*. It is her Christian faith that implied her to remark:

> Little can we sympathize
> With what the Brahman sage would fain imply
> As the concluding moral of his tale,
> That for the hermit-king it was a sin
> To Love his nursling. What! A sin to love!
> A sin to pity! Rather should we deem
> Whatever Brahmans wise, or monks may hold,
> That he had sinned in *casting off* all love
> By his retirement to the forest shades;
> For that was to abandon duties high,
> And, like a recreant soldier, leave the post
> Where God had placed him as a sentinel. (pp. 105-06)

And again:

> Not in seclusion, not apart from all,
> Not in a place elected for its peace,
> Rent in the heat and bustle of the world,
> 'Mid sorrow, sickness, suffering and sin,
> Must be still labour with a loving soul
> Who strives to enter through the narrow gate. (p. 106)

Although such comments are rare in *Ancient Ballads*, it can't be denied that the poetess's Christian sense of service and piety has intruded upon the original story.

In another legend, "Buttoo", the pupil's self-sacrifice is commendable and reminds the reader of the noble Christian sense of resignation to the supreme will of God. Read in this light, the following lines are particularly pertinent:

> Glanced the sharp knife one moment high,
> The severed thumb was on the sod,
> There was no tear in Buttoo's eye,
> He left the matter with his God. (p. 124)

In truth, the 'self-help' (p. 124) of which Toru speaks in the last line of the poem is more relevant to the Christian world than to the Hindu.

With reference to the poem, "The Tree of Life". Mr. Govin Dutt copies as follows from his memorandum book for Mary Martin—it is dated as far back as April 16, 1877—"Yester evening when the candle were lighted, Toru told me, in very low whispers and with some agitation, a dream or vision which she had the day previous about 9 or 10 A.M. She was not asleep at all, but quite awake. I know now why she asked me the evening before, where the text was, 'And I will give thee a crown of life'....[7] "Obviously, the Angel that appeared before Toru's eyes should have been the vision of the Holy Spirit. The vision confirms the reality of death, for which Toru should be fully prepared without any fear, for the *Bible* says: "Do not fear what you are about to suffer. Behold, the devil is about to throw some of you into prison, that you may be tested, and for ten days you will have tribulation."[8] In fact, the very title of the poem is taken from the *Bible* and one may read the following in this context: "And out of the ground the Lord God made to grow every tree that is pleasant to the sight and good for food, the tree of life also in the midst of the garden, and the tree of the knowledge of good and evil."[9]

In "Sonnet-Baugmaree", we have the reference to "a primeval Eden" (p. 171). That the poetess compared her own garden with the garden in Eden shows her deep readings in the *Bible* and her leaning towards the Christian world. Her poems on French and French affairs also cement this belief. We know that she often talked of going away from Indian and settling in England. Thus, in one of her letters to Mary Martin she wrote: "We hope to go to England. I do not know if we shall be able to go; this time Papa says he will sell all we have here and go to England and settle there for good."[10]

The poem, "Sonnet—The Lotus", has also some classical allusions to the western myths goddesses—'Flora', 'Juno' and 'Psyche' (p. 172). These allusions indicate that Toru's mind was saturated with the western images and ideas and that she could never forget the beloved West with its enchantment of frost and snow, its delicate landscapes and its vivid and eager College life. In comparison with the stir and bustle of the West, the days in India seemed monotonous and without event. So in the midst of the profuse splendors of the East says Mr. Fisher, her thoughts "continually reach out to that other home beyond the Ocean, which travel and study had made so dear to her, as, for example, to world (known only through books) of the Bronte sisters, living 'among the lonely wild moors of Yorkshire, all three so full of talent, yet living so solitary amid those Yorkshire wolds', or to the days which stood out with such cameo-like distinctness in her memory, when she enjoyed the free life of a student by the bank of the Cam, passing 'nice cosy evenings' with her friend, and on Sundays drinking deep draughts of music from the college organ".[11]

Hindu Thought

Toru's Christian faith does not conflict with her fascination for the 'deep magics' of Hindu religion and epics. She was, in fact, "a Hindu as well as a Christian".[12] She was, after all, an Indian woman writing in English and in spirit was one with India's woman-singers of the past. She had long been in search of roots and ultimately, found them in the ancient myths and legends of her own land. She agreeably responded to the heart-beats of the antique racial tradition. Her mother was an incentive to her in this. She fired the religious feelings in her daughter, telling the stories from the Hindu scriptures. Later readings in the original Sanskrit gave a keener poetic edge to Toru's delicate sensibility. It is in *Ancient Ballads* that her attraction to the motherland is most pronounced. The old ballads, full of heroism and pathos, provided her a chance to have links with the living past of India and she cared not if Christian or sceptic cavilled at her. After narrating the story of the Goddess Uma who received shell-bracelets from a wandering pedlar, Toru disarmingly adds:

> Absurd may be the tale,
> Ill-suited to the marching times,
> I loved the lips from which it fell,
> So let it stand among my rhymes. (p. 100)

Her love of Hinduism may be clearly sensed in the stories collected in *Ancient Ballads*.

Now something about "Hindu thought'. It is, as we know, mostly based on the *Vedas*, the *Upanishads*, the *Gita* and the *Puranas*. The two great epics—the *Ramayana* and the *Mahabharata*—are also an integral part of Hinduism. Indian philosophers have always advocated a negative approach to human life and God. It is this which distinguishes Hindu thought from Western thought. In this respect, one is tempted to quote Albert Schweitzer: "The Indian Aryans show an inclination to world and life negation, the Iranian-Persian and the European Aryans lean to world and life affirmation. This difference of attitude had its origin in events, and these were reflected in thought."[13] By the European Aryans' what Mr. Schweitzer means is the people living in Europe or Christians. The cardinal trends of Hindu thought are: pessimism, suffering, disinterestedness, other worldliness, the practice of *Yoga*, renunciation, spiritual discipline, etc.[14]

Let us now take up *Ancient Ballads* and examine it in the light of Hindu thought perhaps the most articulate expression of Vedantism—that there is only one God and that this world is as unsubstantial as a shadow—is to be found in "Savitri" in the discourse of Savitri and Yama. This is what Savitri says:

I know that in this transient world
All is delusion,—nothing true:
I know its shows are mists unfurled
To please and Vanish. To renew
Its subtle joys, be magic bound
In *Maya's* network frail and fair,
Is not my aim; The gladsome sound
Of husband, brother, friend, is air
The such as know that all must die,
And that at last the time must come,
When eye shall speak no more to eye
And Love cry,—to, this is my sum. (pp. 66-67)

These lines have a mellowness and a profoundly of thought rarely to be had in Toru's poetry. Here is yet another maxim in the same poem:

I know in such a world as this
No one can gain his heart's desire,
Or pass the years in perfect bliss;
Like gold we must be tried by fire. (p. 67)

Vedantic ideas are to be found also in "Buttoo". This is how Buttoo reveals his firm determination to achieve a unique skill in archery:

And I shall do my best to gain
The science that will not teach,
For life is as a utmost goal we reach
To which the soul prints. I shall try
To realize my waking dream,
And what if I should chance to die?
None miss one bubble from a stream. (p. 115)

Lines 3, 7 and 8 in the above passage are specially to be marked out for Vedantic thought. Another Hindu aphorism is to be had in the following lines of "Savitri":

Of all the pleasures given on earth
    The company of the good is best,
For weariness has never birth
    In such a commerce sweet and blest;
The sum runs on its wonted course.
    The earth its plenteous treasure yields,
All for their sake, and by the force
    Their prayer united ever wields;
On let me, let me ever dwell
    Amidst the good, where'er it be,
Whether in lowly hermit-cell
    Or in some spot beyond the sea. (pp. 71-72)

One of the Upanishadic ideas is contained in the following lines of "Savitri":

And then the inner man was tied
    The soul no bigger than the thumb. (p. 64)

The 'inner man' mentioned heroin is *Jivatma.*

A part from Vedantic ideas, we have also the theory of *Karma* beautifully propounded in *Ancient Ballads.* The following extract from "Savitri" may be quoted here to vindicate the statement:

And each shall suffer as he acts
    And thinks,—his own sad burden bear:
No friends can help,—his sins are facts
    That nothing can annul or spare,
And he must beat their consequence. (p. 67)

The doctrine of *Karma* has been highlighted in the following passage of "Dhruva" too:

    The deeds that thou hast done,
The evil, haply, in some former life,
Long, long ago, who may alas; annul,

Or who the good works not done, supplement;
The sins of previous lives must bear their fruit;
The ivory throne, the umbrella of gold,
The best steed, and the royal elephant
Rich caparisoned, must be his by right
Who has deserved them by his virtuous acts
In times long past. Oh think on this my son,
And be content. For glorious actions done
Not in this life, but in some previous birth,
Suruchee by the monarch is beloved. (pp. 109-10)

The doctrine of *Karma* goes with the belief in the previous lives. This is what we find in the passage. The ballad of "Sindhu" also affirms it. In that ballad, Sindhu tells Dasarath that he is now dying "a bloody death" (p. 135) because in the previous birth he had killed, with his sling and ball, a male dove.

The highest sacrifice made for the practice if spiritual discipline is to be seen in "Dhruva", where the prince of that name leaves princely facilities at home and goes out to the woods. This is Dhruva declaring to his own mother:

Let Uttama my brother,—thy son,—
Receive the throne and royal titles,—all
My father pleases to confer on him,
I grudge that not. Not with another's gifts
Desire I, dearest mother, to be rich,
But with my own work would acquire a name. (p. 112)

And, finally he did achieve the whole true mission of his life.

In "Prahlad", there are references to the Brahmins (p. 143), the holy *Vedas,* (pp. 143-44) and the pundits (p. 144). The speeches of the youthful Prahlad are couched in term of energy and faith. His father asks him where his God is and what looks like and why He does not come down to help his devotee. The young boy looks round, bewildered yet full of faith:

> Hath He a shape, or hath He none?
> I know not this, nor care to know,
> Dwelling in light, to which the sun
> Is darkness.—He sees all below,
> Himself unseen; In him I trust,
> He can protect me if He will,
> And if this body turn to dust,
> He can new life again instill. (p. 155)

The unflinching faith of a Hindu *bhakta* has been beautifully brought out in this passage,—the *bhakta* whose story still lives on the lips of the Indian people, inspiring and instructing them in moments of a spiritual crisis.

Different Hindu Ideals in *Ancient Ballads*

In order to be able to fully appreciate Toru's view of life, one has to take into account the different Hindu ideals represented in *Ancient Ballads and Legends of Hindustan*. The exposition of these ideals might tempt the reader to believe that the poetess had a propensity for didacticism. It is true that she occasionally resorted to preachings in the volume, but since she did her job through the medium of old ballads and legends, the charge is partly attenuated. Perhaps the themes of antiquity that she handled needed them.[15]

It is but natural that the Hindu ideal of womanhood should have appealed to Toru most and in her "Savtiri" she has sung the praise of that great heroine of Hindu mythology. The story and the exalted ideals embedded in it are too familiar to Indians to need any detailed treatment here. It is enough to point out here that Savitri's absolute and whole-hearted devotion to her husband and its ultimate triumph over the merciless God of Death, who is determined to snatch him away from her, are memorable events in themselves. When following her husband, 'to cross the doleful lake' she is asked to retrace her steps homeward and perform the duties of a widow enjoined by the

Shastras. But she is resolute and moves forward on the path of duty without caring for the temptations held forth to her. Even when:

> Pale, pale, the stars above them burned,
> More weird the scene had grown and wild. (p. 64)

She says with indomitable courage and resoluteness:

> No weariness, O death, I feel,
> And how should I, when by the side
> Of Satyavan? In woe and weal
> To be a help mate swears the bride. (p. 69)

In fact, Savitri is an ideal wife and is not ready to leave her husband in woe or weal. Earlier, she had shown the same kind of courage in the face of her parents and Narad Muni in the choice of her future lord and had declared:

> I cannot break
> A plighted faith,—I can not bear
> A wounded conscience. (p. 44)

And again:

> Unwedded to my dying day
> I must, my father dear, remain;
> 'Tis well, if so thou will'st, but say
> Can man balk Fate, or break its chain? (p. 47)

Hindu ideals of Duty are delineated with considerable power in each of this series of ballads,[16] including "Savitri". The heroine of the ballad says:

> Wher'er my husband dear is led,
>
> Or journeys of his own free will,
> I too must go, though darkness spread

Across my path, portending ill,
'Tis thus my duty I have read. (p. 65)

Savitri knows her duty very well and is doing what a virtuous woman should.

If "Savitri" embodies the ideal wife, "Lakshman" gives us the ideal Hindu brother.[17] Lakshman loves Rama from the core of his heart. He is perfectly obedient to the elder brother, seeking glory in faithful service, 'in life-long loyalty and truth'. He is forced by the unwarranted and unkind insinuations of his brother's wife, the heroine of the *Ramayana*, to leave her alone in the forest and go to the help of Rama. He first tries to convince her of Rama's indomitable power, and asks:

What being of demonian birth
Could ever brave his mighty arm?
Is there a creature on the earth
That dares to work our hero harm? (p. 83)

But Sita grows all the more insistent and uses harsh words for him, doubting his motive and character. She says to him:

Learn this,—whatever comes may come,
But I shall not survive my Love,—
Of all my thoughts here is the sum. (p. 86)

Lakshman is now unable to bear such biting words and decides to go to the forest. But before he goes out, he tells Sita:

In going hence I disregard
The plainest orders of my chief,
A dead for me,—a sȯldier,—hard
And deeply painful. (p. 87)

Even while going out, he does not forget to do his duty—the protection of Sita—assigned to him by Rama. He draws a magic circle on the ground asking Sita not to cross it. But we know that Sita violates his instructions and is kidnapped by the king of Lanka, resulting in the fierce battle between Rama and Ravana.

In "The Royal Ascetic and the Hind", we have the clash of two ideals—asceticism and love.[18] The king Bharat, a great ascetic, becomes a great lover of a hind under unavoidable circumstances and forgets altogether about Eternity and God. At the time of his death, too, he is busy thinking of the hind and not of higher issues:

> To it devoted was his last, last thought,
> Reckless of present and of future both! (p. 105)

In the clash of the two ideals, thus, love triumphs over stern asceticism.

But "Dhruva" reverses the order in the clash between the twin forces of love and asceticism. The young boy, having been denied the love of his father due to the interference of his step-mother, decides to pursue the virtuous path:

> I shall try
> The highest good, loftiest place to win
> Which the whole world deems priceless and desires.
> (p. 111)

Leaving behind the palace of his parents, he goes out to the forest and practices penances and offers prayers and attains immortality.

"Buttoo" is the story of the ideal disciple. Being born in a low family, he is rejected by the great Dronacharya as a pupil in archery. Still Buttoo carries on his private practice, in a remote spot until he achieves perfection. Arjuna becomes jealous of him and instigates the master to have Buttoo's thumb as his due as a *guru*. Buttoo, on being so demanded, offers his thumb to his inspirer instantaneously:

> Glanced the sharp knife one moment high,
> The severed thumb was on the sod,

There was no tear in Buttoo's eye,
He left the matter with his God. (p. 124)

Drona is deeply moved by the pupil's sacrifice and prophesies fame and immortality for him in the ages to come. In truth, Buttoo's exemplary conduct is a lesson to all the modern disciples.

From the ideal disciple, we pass in "Sindhu" to the story of the ideal son. While the young boy is filling his pitcher in the evening twilight on the banks of the Saryu River in order to quench the thirst of his adored parents, he is shot by mistake by Dasarath, the great king of Ayodhya. As the whizzing arrow brings Sindhu down to the ground, he cries out in the last agony of death. And on regaining consciousness he gives expression to the noblest sentiments that can ever fall from the lips of a dutiful son:

"And so I die—a bloody death—
    But not for this I mourn,
To feel the world pass with my breath
    I gladly could have borne,"
But for my parents, who are blind,
    And have no other stay,—
This, this weighs sore upon my mind,
    And fills me with dismay". (p. 135)

Thereafter this dutiful boy passes away:

In "Prahlad", there is again the boy chafing under the ill-treatment of his royal father, who is highly tyrannical and proud and who does not like the prayers being offered to God. The father has instructed the tutor not to teach his sons anything about God and the soul. But Prahlad pays no heed to such instructions, as he has firm faith in God and His omnipresence. The ideal devotee that Prahlad has accepted the challenge of his unwise father when the letter asks him to show that his God is in the crystal pillar standing by. Kasyapu, the father, spurns the pillar with his foot and it falls down. From within this pillar appears a stranger but strong warrior, who is half-man and half-lion (*Narasimha*). He gives a shout and strikes the tyrant on the head and tears him into pieces. He hails Prahlad as the 'king of all the realms' and disappears in a thunder-clap. Thus, the ways of God to man have been fully vindicated.

"Sita" presents the picture of an ideal Indian woman.[19] She bears all the tortures of an envious world around her and is exiled by her husband for no guilt of hers. She does not complain of it and simply weeps at the unmerited treatment meted out to her. In fact, she is an epitome of fortitude and temperance.

Thus, we see that *Ancient Ballads* is a volume in which Toru's view of life, her philosophical ideals and various Hindu ideals find a beautiful outlet.

NOTES

1. Harihar Das, *The Life and Letters of Toru Dutt,* p. 65.
2. Quoted in Harihar Das's *Life and Letters,* p. 11.
3. *Ibid.*, p. 63.
4. *Ibid.*, p. 98.
5. *Ibid.*, p. 64.
6. K.R.S. Iyengar, *Indian Writing in English,* p. 64.
7. Harihar Das, *The Life and Letters of Toru Dutt,* p. 339, f.n.
8. "Revelation" (II. 10), *The Bible,* revised standard version New York, Glasgow and Toronto: William Collins Sons & Co. Ltd., 1952), p. 228.
9. "Genesis" (II, 9), *ibid.* p. 2.
10. Harihar Das, *op. cit.*, p. 60.
11. H.A.L. Fisher, "Foreword", *The Life and Letters of Toru Dutt,* ed. Harihar Das, p. IX.
12. Y.N. Vaish, "Toru Dutt", *The Modern Review* (December 1966), p. 437.
13. Albert Schweitzer, *Indian Thought and Its Development* (London: Adam & Charles Black, 1956), p. 3.
14. Dr. Amar Dwivedi's published doctoral dissertation, *Indian Thought and Tradition in T.S. Eliot's Poetry* (Meerut University, 1973), p. 240.

15. A.N. Dwivedi, ed. *Ancient Ballads and Legends of Hindustan*, p. 90.
16. Toru Dutt (Madras: Natesan & Co. 1917), pp. 20-21.
17. *Ibid.*, p. 23.
18. A.N. Dwivedi, *op. cit.*, p. 91.
19. *Ibid.*, p. 93.

Toru Dutt: The Pioneer of Indian English Poetry

8

Toru Dutt was the first great Indian woman writing in English who brought, through her wonderful literary activities, the East and the West close to each other. An Indian by birth and a European by her training, she was best equipped for this noble task. Living in the heart of Calcutta, she used to dream of 'alien shore'. France and England were the ideal places for her to settle in, as some of her letters written to Mary Martin make clear. She was an avid reader of French and English literatures. She expressed her desire to Mlle Clarisse Badar to translate her *La Femme dans I' Inde Antique* and the permission to do so was readily granted.[1] Her *A Sheaf* and *Le Journal* are clear indications of her deep love for French literature and people. Similarly, *Bianca and Ancient Ballads* attest her fascination for the English, though the latter is also a fine, fragrant flower of her fertile imagination fed on native sources. Her literary works themselves are a solid proof of the fact that she stood all for East-West understanding. Her beloved and learned father, her own vast readings and her wide sympathies for the entire mankind: these were the possible factors for fashioning her mind inclined to this kind of understanding.

This attitude of Toru Dutt can be better appreciated today, for the simple fact that the two poles of the globe have now come closer than ever before. There are obvious points of contact between them. They are co-operating with each other in matters of trade and commerce, science and technology, politics and economics, cultural and educational exchanges have become the order of the day. Such an atmosphere is certainly conducive to promoting universal brotherhood and international citizenship.

Toru Dutt was, in the truest sense, a citizen of the world and not of any particular country. In her case, the well-known diction of Rudyard Kipling that 'East is East and West is West/ And never the twain shall meet' becomes meaningless and in fructuous. Mr. Fisher seems to be nearer the truth when he remarks about her thus: "In comparison with the stir and bustle of the West, the days in India seemed monotonous and without event. So in the midst of the profuse splendours of the East her thoughts continually reach out to that other home beyond the Ocean, which travel and study had made so dear to her.... In the long history of the contact interfusion of East and West, I doubt whether there is a figure more encouraging or singnificant."[2]

There is usually made a distinction between the East and the West on the ground that the former is spiritualistic and the latter materialistic Indian thinkers, in the style of Plato, do not take life in piecemeal, but as a whole; in their outlook, both the sides—spiritualistic and materialistic are of equal importance for the development of personality. The distinction, therefore, is not much valid; and if is valid at all, one must remember that Toru's concern was not religious or spiritual, but purely literary, to which end were directed all her energies and fancies. Hers was an exemplary case of literary give-and-take between the two hemispheres of the earth.

The Poetess on the Critics Anvil

Toru Dutt produced a small body of English poetry in her short life on this earth which received a mixed reaction from critics. In the beginning, there were some hurdles in the way of her recognition as a dynamic force in poetry. We know that when the *Sheaf* was ready, no publisher in Calcutta was prepared to bring it out. But when it was anyhow printed and privately published and reached England and fell into the hands of Sir Edmund Gosse, Toru became the cynosure of literary men's eyes. We shall, henceforth, see how Toru and her poetical volumes were received by different cities.

Edmund Gosse was the first critic to review the *Sheaf* sympathetically; his review appeared in *The Examiner*

(August, 1876). Opening the book at random and reading Aru's rendering of Victor Hugo's "Morning Serenade", he was filled with 'surprise and almost rapture'. Later on, he while writing on "Introductory Memoir" to *Ancient Ballads*, called Toru's feat so extraordinary. But he was quick to point out the inequality of the verse in the *Sheaf* and observed:

> The English verse is sometimes exquisite; at other times the rules of our prosody are absolutely ignored, and it is obvious that the Hindu poetess was chanting to herself a music that is discord in an English ear.[3]

So dislodgeable was the opinion of Sir Gosse that almost all subsequent cities of Toru Dutt toed his line. The reviewer of *The English-man*, for instance, adopted the critical tone of Sir Gosse (see chapter II for this). In August, 1879, *The Saturday Review* wrote that there was every reason to believe that intellectual power Toru was one of the most remarkable women that ever lived. Another noted critic, Dunn, thought that Toru was the first of her sex to interpret the soul of India to the West and as such she "struck a genuinely Indian note that reveals the sincerity of a mind proud of the intellectual traditions of its native land".[4] In a scholarly article published in the *Asiatic Review*, Harihar Das spoke highly of the "classical tradition" in Toru's poetry, especially in *Ancient Ballads*. He also wrote, in 1921, the first-ever authentic biography of Toru Dutt (which is now out of print). The great French critic, James Darmester, said of her:

> This daughter of Bengal, so admirably and so strangely gifted, Hindu by race and tradition, an Englishwoman by education, a French woman at heart, poet in English, prose-writer in French; who at the age of eighteen made India acquainted with the poets of France in the rhyme of England, who blended in herself three-souls and three traditions, and died at the age of twenty (*sic*), in the full bloom of her talent and on the eve of the awakening of her genius, presents in the history of literature a phenomenon without parallel.[5]

Dr. Edward Thompson spoke of Toru Dutt and her poetry in the following manner: "The verses grip most of all the vehement soul that they reveal, a soul which has had few fellows throughout time. Toru Dutt remains one of the most astonishing women that ever lived, a woman whose place is with Sappho and Emily Brontë, fiery unconquerable of soul as they...."[6] Another notable man of letters, A.H.L. Fisher had been very generous towards Toru Dutt and his observations about her deserve to be quoted at some length here:

> Toru Dutt was a poet with a rare genius for the acquisition of languages not her own. In her all too brief life she mastered Sanskrit and wrote in France and English with a grace, a facility, and an individual distinction which have given her rank among the authentic voices of Western literature. Her ear, sometimes betrayed her. On points of diction she was not always beyond reproach. Here and there in the *Ancient Ballads and Legends of Hindustan* or in her amazing renderings from the French poets, we come across a word, a phrase, a discord, which reminds us that the poet was not of our race or speech and much the same has been said of her French prose romance by those best qualified to judge of it. Yet when every deduction has been made for unessential blemishes, this child of the green valley of the Ganges has by sheer force of native genius earned for herself the right to be enrolled in the great fellowship of English poets.[7]

The noted Indian critic of English letters, Dr. Amarnatha Jha, presented a judicious account of Toru Dutt and her poetry in his "Introductory Memoir" attached to the Indian edition of *Ancient Ballads*. This is how he sums her up:

> One cannot help regretting that time cut short prematurely a career of such promise and such early fulfillment. There were few poetic glories which, given maturity, she could not have achieved. She could have interpreted to the West the spirit of India and could have brought about a closer and more sympathetic understanding. She might have development into a novelist or a writer of lyrics breathing grace and sweetness. That was not to be. Let us be

> contented that we had this brief visitant in our midst and she remains eternally young, for ever fresh and for ever fair, still dreaming the glittering dreams of youth.[8]

Another sound critic, Dr. K.R. Srinivasa Iyengar, says that Toru "has left behind her a body of achievement to which it will be difficult to find a parallel in the history of English literature".[9] Paying his glowing tributes to Toru Dutt, Mr. Alokeranjan Das Gupta has remarked:

> She was the first of our modern artists who have transmitted the nervous tension of adolescence into the saner idiom of art. In the incredibly short spell of her life, she successfully crystallized the diverse ways of innocence and experience into the supreme moment of Art which is brief, yet abiding.[10]

This is how the sensible woman critic, Padmini Sengupta, responds to Toru Dutt: "In her 'pride in her country's great inheritance, she was Indian to the core'. And she herself has become a heritage of India, bringing renown to her motherland through the arches of the years—a name ever to be remembered. Toru, a frail and exotic blossom which blossomed but for a short while, has left a fragrance which will never die." And, finally, we come to the opinion of yet another Indian scholar, Dr. A.N. Dwivedi, who wrote an article of good length on Toru Dutt and her poetry, at the end of which he observed:

> Obviously, Toru Dutt was the first Indian to handle English verse with ease, freedom and command. Her achievements, both linguistic and technical, were of an excellent order, and when the *Sheaf* first appeared, it was even thought that the author was an Englishman writing under the pseudonym of "Toru Dutt". In fact, Toru Dutt possessed an inborn poetic talent which found its best outlet in the English language.[11]

Taking all these opinions into consideration, it is not difficult to arrive at the conclusion that Toru Dutt has earned for herself the approbation of almost all critics and the condemnation of none. This one-sided tilt in her favour should not lead the reader to construe that even her faults have been glossed over by the critics. Her shortcomings have certainly been aired out but only to indicate the immaturity of her years and the great promise that she showed. Many critics, as may be gathered from the foregoing observations, have overlooked her minor blemishes which would have gone when with the growth of age and with greater practice in poetic art. It is this that Sir Edmund Gosse means when he says that "mellow sweetness" was all that Toru Dutt lacked to perfect her as in English poet and "of no other oriental who has ever lived can the same be said."[12]

Her Place in Indo-Anglian Poetry

Toru's assessment as a poetess is based on her two collections of poetry—*A Sheaf* and *Ancient Ballads*. It is true that her poetic work is meagre, but it is real gem and it has enabled Toru Dutt to carve out for herself a permanent place in English poetry. Prof. Dunn has rightly described her as "the founder of the modern school of English poetry".[13]

As regards her place in Indo-Anglian poetry, it may be said that it is with her that the real beginning in this branch of poetry is made. Her predecessors like Derozio, Kasiprasad and Madhusudan were mere experimentalists in the field. Had she lived longer, she would have produced some more poetry of lasting worth and thereby consolidated her gains. But the saddest thing about her is what she 'might have been'.

Still Toru remains, even today, one of the four 'classics' in Indo-Anglian literature: the other three are Rabindranath Tagore, Sri Aurobindo and Sarojini Naidu. These four may be regarded as the 'four wheels' of Indo-Anglian literature. And of these four Toru's name stands at the top in point of chronology. Toru showed the direction to her successors; Tagore and Sri Aurobindo endowed depth and scope to Indo-Anglian literature; and Mrs. Naidu enriched it with her delightful songs. So, all these four have their own importance in Indo-Anglian literature, but Toru enjoys the privilege of precedence over them.

Sometimes, a comparative study is made between Toru Dutt and Sarojini Naidu and to a certain extent it is valid too. The points of similarity between the two are that both were Indian women writing in English and that both were sponsored by Sir Edmund Gosse. Both Toru and Sarojini are simple in expression, but the former is "more natural" and "more mature"[14] than the latter. Toru did not strive, barring in "Our Casuarina Tree" and the sonnet dedicated to her father, to tell the world about her personal pains and pleasures which Sarojini so vociferously did. Observations of nature of the two writers are also different. To Toru, the trees just happen to be Indian—the trees she loves, but to Sarojini the trees, in order to be Indian, must be described with an Oriental background. Further, the reader comes across a few meaningful utterances in Toru's poetry about the social conditions, dogmas, political states and flatterers, but Sarojini hardly ever tried to understand or reveal human nature.[15] Another important point of contrast between the two poetesses is that Toru Dutt worked ceaselessly till her end, but Sarojini did not produce a systematic work after 1917 and only occasionally retuned to compose her girlish poems in the twenties and thereafter no more. There is deeper thought and feeling in Toru Dutt than in Sarojini Naidu. And to this are added Toru's endless possibilities of reaching an ever-escalating standard of poetic work. But for one thing—the prosodic excellence,—the scale swings, guided by any standards, in favour of Toru Dutt.

Some people find the influence of the Romantic poets, of Browning and Tennyson, on her poetic art. It is only partly true, as she wrote under the dictates of no single poet or school. It is likely that in favour of their arguments they may say that there are many beautiful and long descriptions of natural scenes and sounds in her poetry and that she, while making the selection for her rendering in the *Sheaf*, showed an inclination towards the French Romanticists. But these are only arguments to substantiate a preconceived notion and they, as told earlier, do not contain the whole truth. While discussing the *Sheaf*, it has been pointed out that Toru's selection of poets is wide-ranging and not limited, though it is a different matter that the best of French poetry has been written by the Romantic poets. One cannot, therefore, place Toru Dutt in "any water-light category or school of poets".[16] Once in a while, when Nature wearies of her own uniformity and rigidity, she throws up a rare and exotic phenomenon like Toru Dutt.

Toru, in fact, stands out as a pride of the nineteenth century India, illumination her literary galaxy. But she is much more than that. She is perfect fulfillment of the hopes and aspirations of noble English people who came out to India with a genuine desire to help this unhappy land of promise to reach her destined greatness and also a sure warning against the futile attempt of grafting an alien culture and civilization on a land grossly misunderstood. We cannot think of a greater fulfillment than in her of the high moral qualities, of the unshakable faith in Jesus, of the intellectual attainments of Europe's best minus her sciences. She has been characterized as a "great daughter of India, holy as a white lotus, sweet as a rose, who...enjoyed the beauty of the sky and air, redolent of myrrh instead of the tulasi".[17] The only objection here is that Toru was as well a 'myrrh' as a 'tulasi'. The latter is taken as a token of the soul of India and it is next to impossible that a person of Toru's sensibility should remain oblivious of the soul that produced her. *Ancient Ballads* is a living example of it. Taking this fact into account, it is natural for us to subscribe to the view of an enlightened Bengali critic who proudly remembers Toru Dutt as "this prestige-child of our culture".[18]

As a poetess, Toru has never been 'forsaken'. There is hardly another English writer in India who is so regularly remembered in the journals and newspapers of the country. In India's *who's who*, she figures among the great. Neither are her biographers in English, Bengali and French scarce. She has certainly passed the test of time and is still very much alive, proving herself a 'classic' writer. It is, therefore, difficult to agree those who treat her as 'a dead-horse'. On the contrary, she has almost always found a place in an anthology of Indo-Anglian poetry and right from her own days, some of her poems, notably "My Vocation", "Our Casuarina Tree", "The Lotus", "The Sonnet—Baugmaree", "Savitri", "Lakshman", etc. have been prescribed in the syllabi of schools, colleges and universities. Is it not a soiled proof of her living greatness? She has decidedly created a permanent place for herself in English poetry. The learned critic, Sir Edmund Gosse, is quite correct when he observes thus: "when the history of the literature of our country comes to be written, there is sure to be a page in it dedicated to this fragile exotic blossom of song".[19] And the observation has come true, as we do find a page dedicated to Toru Dutt in George Sampson's *The Concise Cambridge History of English Literature* (914). She has, thus, come to occupy her legitimate place in the annals of English letters and no detractor can dislodge her from there:

> A lily of a day
> Is fairer far in May,
> Although it fall and die that night,—
> It was the plant and flower of Light,
> In small proportions we just beauties see,
> And in short measures life may perfect be.
>
> Ben Johnson

NOTES

1. "Appendix I" to Mr. Das's *Life and Letters of Toru Dutt,* pp. 350-51.
2. H.A.L. Fisher, "Foreword", *The Life and Letters,* p. ix.
3. Edmund Gosse, "Introductory Memoir", *Ancient Ballads,* pp. xv-vi.
4. T.O.D. Dunn, *The Bengali Writers of English Verse,* p. 22.
5. Quoted in Mr. Das's *Life and Letters*, p. 1.
6. "Supplementary Review", *The Life and Letters,* p. 344.
7. "Foreword", *The Life and Letters,* p. vii.
8. A. Jha, "Introductory Memoir", *Ancient Ballads,* p. 36.
9. A. Dasgupta, "This Fragile Exotic Blossom of Songs", *Indian Literature,* IX, No. 2 (April-June 1966), 14.
10. P. Sengupta, *Toru Dutt* (1968), p. 86.
11. A.N. Dwivedi, "Toru Dutt and Her Poetry", *WLWE,* 14, No. 2 (November 1975), 289.
12. E. Gosse, "Introductory Memoir", *Ancient Ballads,* p. xxvii.
13. Dunn, *The Bengali Writers of English Verse*, p. 20.
14. Padmini Sengupta, *Sarojini Naidu* (New Delhi: Sahitya Akademi, 1974), p. 95.

15. *Ibid.*, p. 96.
16. Najoo Bilimoria, "Toru Dutt: Beloved of the Gods", *The Illustrated Weekly of India* (March 4, 1956), p. 64.
17. Radhakamal Mukerjee, "Toru Dutt", *Great Women of India,* ed. Swami Madhavananda and Ramesh Chandra Majumdar (Mayavati, Almora, Himalyas: Advaita Ashram, 1953), p. 403.
18. Quoted from a letter, dated March 25, 1975 that Dr. Prithwindranath Mukerjee, the translator of *Le Journal,* wrote from Paris to me.
19. Gosse, "Introductory Memoir", *Ancient Ballads*, p. xxvii.

Bibliography

(A) PRIMARY SOURCES

Dutt, Toru. *A Sheaf Gleaned in French Field.* 2nd ed. Bhowanipore: Saptahik Sambad Press, 1878.

——. *Ancient Ballads and Legends of Hindustan.* London: Kegan Paul, 1882. Two Indian editions have come out so far, one edited by A.N. Jha (Allahabad: Kitabistan, 1941) and the other by Dr. A.N. Dwivedi (Bareilly: Prakash Book Depot, 1976.

——. *Bianca, or Young Spanish Maiden.* Serialized in the *Bengal Magazine,* VI, Jan.-Apr. 1878.

——. *Le Journal de Medemoiselle d' Arvers.* Paris: Didier, 1879. It has been rendered into Bengali and English.

——. *Essays* (Two). *The Bengal Magazine,* Dec. 1874.

——. *A Scene from Contemporary History. The Bengal Magazine,* June-July 1875.

——. Letters to Miss Mary Martin and Mlle. Clarisse Bader Published in Hariher Das's *The Life and Letters of Toru Dutt.* London: Oxford Univ. Press, 1921.

(B) SECONDARY SOURCES

(i) Books

Aurobindo, Sri. *The Renaissance in India.* Pondicherry: Sri Aurobindo Ashram, 1973.

Basu, Lotika. *Indian Writers of English Verse.* Calcutta: The Univ. Press, 1933.

Dunn, T.O.D. *The Bengali Writers of English Verse.* Bombay: Longmans, Green & Co., 1918.

Dutts, Govin, Omesh, Greece and Hur. *The Dutt Family Album*. London: Longmans, Green & Co., 1870.

Dwivedi, A.N. *Toru Dutt*, New Delhi: Arnold-Heinemann, 1977.

Frazer, R.W. *Literary History of India*. London: T. Fisher Unwin, 1898.

Iyengar, K.R.S. *Indian Contribution to English Literature*. Bombay: Karnataka Publishing House, 1945.

——. *Indian Writing in English*. Bombay: Asia Publishing House, 1973.

Kotoky, P.C. *Indo-English Poetry*. Gauhati: The Univ. Publication Dept., 1969.

Macnicol, Margaret. *Poems by Indian Women*. Calcutta: Y.M.C.A. Press and London: O.U.P., 1923.

Majumdar, R.C., *et al., British Paramountcy and Indian Renaissance,* X, part II. Bombay: Bhartiya Vidya Bhavan, 1965.

Narasimhaiah, C.D. *The Swan and the Engle*. Shimla: Indian Institute of Advanced Study, 1969.

Nurullah, Syed and Naik, J.P., *A Student's History of Education in India*: 1800-1947. Rev. ed. Bombay: Macmillan, 1947.

Sengupta, Padmini. *Toru Dutt*. New Dehli: Sahitya Akadem, 1968.

——. *Sarojni Naidu*. New Delhi: Sahitya Akad., 1974.

Toru Dutt: A Sketch of Her Life and on Appreciation of Her Work. 2nd ed. Madras: G.A. Natesan & Co., 1917.

(ii) Articles

Dasgupta, Alokernjan. "This Fragile Exotic Blossom of Songs", *Indian Literature,* IX, No. 2 (April-June 1966), pp. 6-14.

Das Gupta, Jyotis Chandra "Toru Dutt", *National Biography for India,* IV (1914), pp. 297-310.

Das, Harithar. "Classical Tradition in Toru Dutt's Poetry", *Asiatic Review* (Oct. 1931), pp. 695-715.

Dwivedi, A.N. "Toru Dutt and Her Poetry", *World Literature Written in English*, 14, No. 2 (Nov. 1975), pp. 278-90.

——. "Toru Dutt and Sarojini Naidu", *Commonwealth Quarterly* (Dec. 1978).

The Examiner, August 26, 1876.

Gowda, H.H. Anniah. "Toru Dutt and Sarojini Naidu as Poets", *The Literary Half-Yearly,* IX, No. 1 (1968), pp. 19-30.

Iyengar, K.R.S. "Indian Writing in English", *Contemporary Indian Literature.* Rev. and enlarged ed. New Delhi: Sahitya Akademi, 1959.

Mitra, Dipemndranath. "The Writing of Toru Dutt", *Indian Literature,* IX, No. 2 (Apr.-June 1966), pp. 33-38.

Mukerjee, Kalipada. "Toru Dutt and Her Work", *The Calcutta Review,* XLIII (Apr.-June 1932), pp. 197-204.

Mukerjee, Radhakamal. "Great Indian Women of the Nineteenth Century", *Great Women of India,* eds. Swami Madhavananda and R.C. Majumdar, Mayavati, Almora, Himalayas: Advaita Ashram, 1953, pp. 399-403.

Mukerjee, S.V. "Toru Dutt", *Disjecta Membra.* Banglore: The Institute of World Culture, 1959.

The Saturday Review, August 1879.

Sethusavitri, R. "Indian Writers of English Verse: (1) Toru Dutt", *The Literary Criterion,* III (Winter 1953), pp. 33-41.

Talookdar, B.K. "The Poetry of Toru Dutt", *Journal of the University of Bombay,* IV, Part 6 (May 1936), pp. 71-90.

Vaish, Y.N. "Toru Dutt", *The Modern Review* (Dec. 1966). pp. 436-39.

(iii) Letters

Mitra, Dipendranath. New Delhi, dated Nov. 30, 1973.

Mukherjee, Prithwindranath. Paris, dated March 25, 1974.